ONE PILGRIM'S STORY

To Jo –
a fellow pilgrim

Fr Aidan
Dec 09

ONE PILGRIM'S STORY
A PERSONAL DISCOVERY
OF THE VIA FRANCIGENA

AIDAN SHARRATT

Matthew James Publishing

First published in the UK in 2009 by
Matthew James Publishing Ltd
19 Wellington Close
Chelmsford
Essex CM1 2EE

www. matthew-james.co.uk

ISBN 978-1-898366-93-5

A catalogue record for this book is available from the British Library

Cover Design by Gill England
Design and typesetting by Michael Shaw

Text set digitally in Sabon

Printed in England by Cromwell Press Group,
via MBC Print Consultancy

Contents

Acknowledgements

My thanks to all those who encouraged and helped me in my exploration of the Medieval Pilgrim Route through Italy. Thanks first to Westminster Diocese who gave me a sabbatical (I like to think I'd earned it.)

Family and friends know that I am grateful, but I should mention Betty G. who provided a safe home for my precious books and kept my possesions (and me) in order.

Ann T. of the British Library gave expert advice on ancient sources of information. Where things are accurate, that will be her work. When it came to writing the book there are those who worked harder than I did; Margaret E. who made sense of my chaotic notes, my brother Peter who edited the whole text and advised on illustrations. Michael Shaw who honed and pruned things further and made it into book form. From both of these I was grateful to receive advice as to what you can and cannot include in a book. There are others whose names I shall not write here, but, now that the book is published, they will hear from me.

There are as many pilgrim routes through Italy as there are ancient roads and Jerusalem is not their only goal. Groups from one part or another joined or left the main North to South Roman road system between the Alps and the heel of Italy according to where they came from and where they were aiming for.

On my journey I suppose I walked well over 900 miles; in fact a thousand times a thousand paces, in the Roman way of counting (Milia Passum) Recently a man called Napoleon Bonaparte changed all that and for two centuries, distances in Italy have been marked in Kilometers, though I saw not a few stones marked in Roman Miles along the way

On my journey I did not walk against the clock or in competition with anyone. I'm used to the very ordinary pace of 20 miles a day, but I will happily do more or less according to what is ahead of me.

I took several breaks on the way as pilgrims used to do before they became packaged pilgrims.

I also did the whole route on foot, starting each section exactly where I had left off before.

I recommend travelling on foot. It is increasingly popular today, for instance on the road to Santiago de Compostella.

To walk is to be in touch both with a land and its people, and I was more than happy to depend on those I met, and bring out that innate kindness which is in every Italian. I felt closer to the medieval pigrim too. Most of them walked, though some of the menfolk had donkeys (not so the women and the poor).

I was threatened with extreme violence only once, near Carrara, when I suggested to a drunkard that he might like to stop smashing up a telephone box.

Was I personally on a pilgrimage? Well I may have intended to remain detached and objective, but what began as a study became a personal journey.

John Bunyan introduced his Pilgrim's Progress as the "The similitude of a Dream", and though I did begin as he did by struggling through the Slough of Despond my journey was no allegory.

I had started with a determination to fulfil a task. Without my knowing it my will and desire had turned to love.

"L'amor che move il sole e l'altre stelle"
(Dante Paradiso. XXXIII.145.)

Via Francigena

Preparation for a Pilgrimage

In the spring of 959 the frozen corpse of Bishop Aelfsige was found on the slopes of the Gran San Bernado. He was Bishop of Winchester and had been promoted to the See of Canterbury and so he set off for Rome to collect his *Pallium* (a woollen stole the pope bestowed on metropolitan archbishops), and in the depth of winter he had attempted to cross the pass.

Peace be upon his Saxon bones.

Many pilgrims from northern Europe did succeed in walking to Rome or even to Bari in the heel of Italy, and from there set sail for the Holy Land. From Canterbury to Rome it is over 1,000 miles. Benet Biscop, founder of monasteries, journeyed from Jarrow in Northumbria in the seventh century, back and forth to Rome six times, collecting manuscripts to be copied, and once, it is said, he carried his mother there pick-a-back. Bishops, monks, pilgrims, soldiers, merchants, con-men and saints, they were all waiting for me to catch up with them along the *Via Francigena*, each with a different tale to tell.

"Via Francígena" (the Road of Frankish Origin), had occupied my mind for years, and I was determined one day to walk at least the Italian section from the Swiss border to the heel of Italy. Then, after thirty-five years working as a priest in Westminster Diocese, London, I was offered a Sabbatical Year, a time for renewal. I decided to walk from the Gran San Bernado to the heel of Italy along the Medieval Pilgrim Routes.

The walking would scarcely take three months, I would have time to visit friends, and villages I have known, in over forty years of travelling in Italy, to stay in monasteries, and to fit in some art-study courses in Florence and Siena .

I intended to do the whole route on foot, something like 900 miles, but there would also be time to explore alternative routes, and to visit other places of pilgrimage. – At each point where I left the road I would place five small stones as markers and when I resumed I would start again exactly from that point.

In the tiny chapel of Saint Eldrado at Novalesa on the Moncensio Pass there is a fresco of the investiture of this pilgrim saint. The abbot places a warm tunic over the pilgrim's head, a monk hands him his pilgrim's staff, a small bag made of skin lies ready to be filled with food for the journey. Pilgrims were like an Order; they had a uniform and there was a parting ceremony before they began their journey. Friends would give messages, request prayers and provide money. The pilgrim might wear a badge, a palm for Jerusalem, a shell for Santiago de Compostella. Most wore a large hat (*petasum*), broad-rimmed against the sun, and used a long metal-tipped staff for support, and as protection against brigands.

A medieval pilgrim could expect to be away for at least three years. Many who set out were never heard of again, at least not in their own home town.

In various ways, in my own parish of St. Thomas More, Manor House, and with my family, I had gone through these meaningful rituals of departure, and in January 2003 I was lifted up on wings and transported to Rome where I intended to complete the research on this pilgrim route which I had done in the British Library, London, by spending a few days at the Italian National Library in Rome. I learnt to bless that company of enthusiasts, the 'Roméi' (pilgrims to Rome), who, in the years leading up to the Jubilee of 2000 A.D., diligently traced the ancient pilgrim routes and published their findings. Building on their efforts, I could now plot my walk through Aosta, Piemonte, Lombardy, Emilia,

Tuscany, and Lazio to Rome, and on through the Campania to Apulia.

Enough of books for the time being; I left Rome and went east into the Simbruini hills to the Benedictines of Subiaco. Here, at Santa Scolastica, hard by the Sacro Specco where St. Benedict was torn between his desire for solitude and his calling to be the leader of a great movement, I stayed for three weeks with the silent monks. For a welcome no words were necessary, and there was warmth even at minus 6° C.

My starting-point was to be in the far North West of Italy, but first I visited the desert island of San Francesco in the lagoon of Venice where the spirit of Francis, that "other Christ" and tireless pilgrim, still lives on.

Now I was impatient for the mountain passes of the north west, and it seemed best to limber up for the journey proper by exploring first one other route. The Moncensio Pass, and the steepling Sagra di San Michele, as arduous a mule-track climb as any pilgrim could hope for. And then for a final send-off, I had the hospitality and encouragement of dear friends in Borgo San Dalmazzo near Cuneo, where we talked of peace amid news of preparations for war in the middle east, when, as always, politicians paraded lies for banners.

To Saunter

Where dictionaries refuse to commit themselves the pilgrim is free to point out the obvious.

To 'saunter' is to set out for the Holy Land (*Sainte Terre*). In the middle ages the poor walked, the more comfortable had donkeys or horses, and what all had in abundance was time.

Where was the need for haste?

Modern pilgrims have no concept of what it is to put one foot in front of another, no sense of distance, no sense of achievement.

They are lifted up in a capsule and deposited where they want to be. They carry their own world with them, and are immune to any foreign influence. The shrine, the object of their journey, is consumed along with burger and chips. What is lacking is that they have not sauntered.

More recently, the modern mind has been corrupted by the convention that everything has to be done against the clock, be it an archaeological dig or the wallpapering of a house. If a person goes from A to B, he must do it more quickly than someone else. In Ancient times when they said to Pythagoras "The hero won the race by a whole minute!" he replied, "And what did he do with the minute he had gained?"

Thoughts on the Gran San Bernardo

The Gran San Bernado Pass, rich in history, is well known and was for a long time the most important Alpine Pass. Today it is permanently under-passed by a tunnel, and it hardly takes the trouble to wake up for a couple of months each summer. It is called 'Great' by comparison with the lesser St. Bernard Pass to the West, but, perversely, it is named, not after the Great St. Bernard of Clairvaux (of whom more later), but after the lesser St. Bernard of Menton, ninth-century archdeacon of the Cathedral of Aosta. This compassionate man was moved by the plight of the travellers arriving exhausted in the city and who spoke of their companions who had died on the pass. He upgraded the existing hospice on the pass and now it is the Augustinian Friars who care for those who cross and who provide refuge for them, whether they are in distress or not.

This is the place for legends. In Roman Imperial times it was used by the legions who went "per juga montis Jovina" (over Jupiter's mountain). Where armies go, merchants follow.

Brave Saxons regularly made the journey. In 1050 Sweyn the Bad, brother of King Harold, went by a on guilt-ridden pilgrimage to Jerusalem. He never returned.

In mid-July, 1154, Abbot Nikulaus, of Munkathvera in Iceland, marvelled at the snow and the frozen lakes.

I have in the past been a guest of the Augustinian Canons. Their visitors' book records twenty emperors in seven centuries among whom was Frederick Redbeard.

Generals in every century, not least Napoleon, cursed the blizzards and force-marched their troops over into the promised land of Italy.

But perhaps more than anything it was the Grand Tour which popularised the Gran San Bernado. Between the sixteenth and nineteenth centuries rich northerners risked their lives to cross it. Coaches had to be dismantled and bodily hauled over as they faced every danger from brigands and from the forces of nature.

If we seek documentation and proof, we must visit the museum attached to the hospice: diaries of travellers, etchings and early photos make us understand why Italians thought these German, French and English visitors were eccentric to the point of folly.

When we think of the Great Saint Bernard we must forget all about dogs and think rather of a holy monk from Champagne who led the Cistercians who were at the heart of Church reforms in the eleventh century. He was reluctantly involved in Church politics, preferring to write lyric works on the Bible. His name was 'Doctor Mellifluus' (honey-tongued doctor) and his emblem was a beehive, yet he could sting when attacking abuses in the Church. He was dragooned by the pope into launching the unsuccessful second crusade, and was affectionately known as the last of the ancient Fathers of the Church.

False Start: Nightmare in Aosta: 10th March 2003

The city of Aosta is quietly proud; it is clean and orderly and content with its history. It is also the capital of the one region of Italy I have never visited, and it smiles a welcome as it basks in the winter sun. The little *Hotel Turin* is comfortable and has a view of the surrounding hills.

Everything in my back-pack has been carefully checked and weighed against necessity. My clothes are even over-qualified for the task ahead. Tomorrow I shall go 22 Miles North by bus from Aosta, as near as possible to the snow-blocked border with Switzerland, and from the Italian slopes of the Gran San Bernado I shall begin the long walk South. Nothing can go wrong, I say to myself, as I pull the blankets over my head

At midnight I wake up.

Have I been stabbed? Is this an Incubus, a fateful night-time revelation?

Why are the walls of the room turning in circles and closing in on me? And what is this pain which would make dying seem a happy release? Renal Colic. I've lived with it for well over forty years. By 3.00 a.m. I realise I cannot get out of this on my own. Hotel staff call a doctor and in twenty minutes I am under sedation, and in the morning I awake to find myself, like Dante, unsure and alone.

Nel mezzo del cammin di nostra vita
mi ritrovai per una selva oscura,
che la diritta via era smarrita.

Midway along the journey of our life I woke to find myself in a
dark wood, for I had wandered off from the straight path.

11th **March.** The General Hospital, Aosta, 9.30 a.m. I am sitting in
the Accident and Emergency waiting room. A triage system exists,
but it seems to be operated by the patients themselves, who say
(in French or Italian), "No, No! after you. I'm sure you're more
ill than I am". Have I died and gone to heaven? Or am I simply
among civilised people?

This pilgrim has not yet even made the first faltering steps
of his journey, and already he has experienced hospitality in the
medieval sense. Consultants and tests are arranged for the next two
mornings, but what shall I do with the afternoons?

To do nothing is to worry, and walking is therapy, so I decide to
attempt a 15 mile stage, using Aosta as my base, and so to find out
whether it is wise to continue the long pilgrimage. Or would it be
better to fly back to England and the NHS?

Today, I shall wander round Aosta, which was founded by the
Romans who brought civilisation to the area by slaughtering half
the population and selling the rest into slavery and sinking the prof-
its into a military post with its gateways, walls and theatre. I am
strangely detached: is that the effect of pain-killers or of the uncer-
tainty? Is this pleasant city a starting point for me or a cul-de-sac?
But I know I must at least set out. In the words of D.H. Lawrence,
"Comes over one an absolute necessity to move and, what is more,
to move in some particular direction" (Sea and Sardinia)

At the hospital, the tests have not been arduous, and I have been
topped up with another bottle of saline solution. Late morning,
I take the bus to S. Rémy en Bosses. Where to the left the road
runs towards the tunnel under the Alps to Switzerland; to the right

the road leads to S. Rémy village and the Gran San Bernado Pass. Except that it doesn't. Not at this time of the year.

In the modern village, with its bus station and transport café, I seek out the church and sit there quietly and very much alone, not knowing whether I am making the first steps on a long journey or filling in time before flying back to England.

There I am heartened by the sight of familiar friends, St. Christopher and St. Roch, who quietly nod encouragement. Is it possible we may become fellow pilgrims? For the long-distance pilgrim to Rome this has always been the dilemma: set off on foot from the channel at any time but spring and you will miss the two-month window of opportunity for an Alpine crossing in July and August. But if you choose to cross the Gran San Bernado in the summer months, the journey down to Rome will be made in oppressive heat.

Medieval pilgrims solved the problem by taking their time and waiting patiently until the way was clear for the next stage.

I had made my choice: "In early spring. I will stand on the Italian slopes of the Gran San Bernado and there begin my walk", and this I do today.

The narrow village of S. Rémy, icy and deserted, is hemmed in by steep pine-clad hillsides and everything is covered in snow. I sit on a fallen tree-trunk, and, for no reason, I have a flashback to June 1953, and the coronation of our dear queen, when we were all gathered on the village green and there was a race for the children, and, as a concession to the vertically challenged, I was given twenty yards start, and was cheered to the echo when I came in not quite last. This then will be my starting point.

I stand up, look north for a moment, and salute with awe and reverence the crags above me, and then turn round smartly and set out in the direction of Rome. Whatever may occur, I reason, it is downhill all the way, since I am at the top of Italy and Rome is not.

Half an hour ago I took an extra pain-killer in addition to the other pills I've been given, and I begin to think that life is not so bad after all. Soon the road is entirely ice-free, and is kept that way by passing cars and lorries. I even wave and smile at a kindly motorist who offers me a lift, and I explain that I'm walking to Bari, though to myself I say I've only got to make it to Aosta.

Walking is easy. Today I have only my smaller pack to carry, with water and bread and cheese and a pocket version of Dante as a talisman.

Saint Ouen smiles in the sun, and a woman greets me in French as I enter the village church to reward myself with a little rest, though I have walked only a couple of miles. Ahead of me, round a curve in the valley is the larger and more important Étroubles. Here I begin to sense that I am on a road with a history. The four-lane highway by-passes the ancient town, but I take the straight route along the narrow main street and look up at the houses from whose windows the inhabitants of old saw many a merchant, soldier and pilgrim pass below.

Here Nikulaus of Munkathvera, Abbot of the monastery of Thingor, came through on his way to the Holy Land on 29th July, 1154. "Vir Sapiens et Celeber" (a wise and famous man, qualities rarely twinned), "multisciens prudens et verax" (knowledgeable, prudent and truthful). He had set off by boat from Iceland and then come by land from Norway, writing a diary and an itinerary for future travellers, seeking out churches and hospices and jotting down local lore. He had named the hospice on the pass 'Bjanardz Spitali' and decided to call Étroubles 'Throelabourg'. For the short distance of the main street I am proud to be walking in the shadow of the great man who will be one of my companions on my pilgrimage.

But who is this bishop walking towards me? Can it be Sigeric, another tenth-century Archbishop of Canterbury, proudly show-ing everyone the *pallium* he has just received in Rome from Pope John XV as he returns to his see in England? He too had difficulty with local accents - at one time he thought the people were calling the place 'Praelaporp'.

Encouraged by these encounters, I no longer feel so isolated and can even enjoy the local fountain festooned with icicles. Now Gignod, which is the last stage before Aosta, is visible on a steep mound and it has both a church and a pilgrim shrine. It occurs to me that these villages of Roman origin are spaced perfectly as resting places. In the centuries which interest me, the days of the pilgrimages, the traveller knew he had not yet reached Italy, for this area was under Savoy until very recent times.

> Savoia, in Lingua nostra "salva via"
> vuol dir, pero che salva la strada
> de l'Alpi trala Franza e Lombardia

> (Savoy, in our language "saves the way"
> That means, it protects the Alpine road,
> Between France and Lombardy)

And yet the early writers add that it is neither in France nor Italy: "Negne est in Gallia negne in Italia",

One more hill to skirt. The lights come on during this last hour, and I am now walking on pavements. I can see Augusta Pretoria (Aosta) spread out in the valley below: the remains of the Roman Theatre, a stretch of Roman wall, Santa Maria Assunta, San Pietro, Sant'Orso, a litany of delights interrupted suddenly by the *basso profondo* of a St. Bernard dog, who bashes his head against a garden fence in his efforts to get at me and tear me apart.

Back at the *Hotel Turin* they pay me the compliment of not being over-anxious, and as an act of faith in the future of my pilgrimage I begin a daily reading from Dante's great poem. He was full of foreboding when he began his own pilgrimage in the Holy Year of 1300 and sensed himself "In the middle of a dark wood"

I too am not yet out of the woods. I am unsure of the way ahead. However, the preparation and anticipation are over, and my pilgrimage must begin.

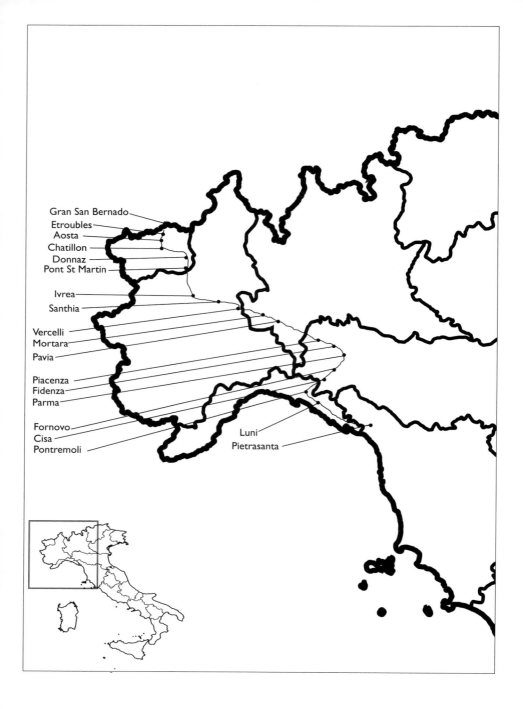

Gran San Bernado
Etroubles
Aosta
Chatillon
Donnaz
Pont St Martin

Ivrea
Santhia

Vercelli
Mortara
Pavia

Piacenza
Fidenza
Parma

Fornovo
Cisa
Pontremoli

Luni
Pietrasanta

From the Gran San Bernardo to Pietrasanta: 11th March to 10th April

In the crypt of the Duomo at morning Mass I ask for the prayers of the good people of Aosta. There are those, such as Canon Goré of the cathedral, who know my intentions and the distance I hope to travel (more than 500 miles to Rome). But, as I leave, one woman asks "which train are you getting to Rome then?" *Magari se fosse vero*! If only it were true.

As I stop to buy bread and cheese for the journey, I hear a middle-aged woman speak of a purchase she made yesterday. "It cost me 120 Denarii", she said, and any passing Roman Legionary would have understood: She had renamed the Euro already. With a similar verbal tenacity, the locals use the classical 'Salve' for a greeting, as they do elsewhere in non-tourist Italy. 'Salve' and 'Ave' are civilised greetings, but they have been ousted by 'Ciao' which has spread like a loathsome infection from the north. In fifteenth-century Venetian dialect 'Ciao' stood for 'Sono Schiavo tuo', I am your slave' This meaningless greeting, as insincere as an air-kiss, is now heard everywhere. Let us get back to the manly honest greetings of the ancients. Did Brutus, as he struck with his republican dagger flap a limp wrist and cry 'Ciao, Caesar'?

Enough. For ease of heart and mind I repair to St. Orso where in the cloister bold carvings are in the style of Burgundy and Provence, and in the sanctuary before the altar lies an early mosaic, a magical word puzzle:

ROTAS

OPERA

TENET

AREPO

SATOR

I notice, for what it's worth, that you can find in it the words Pater Noster, twice over – but I struggle over the lack of one N. Until a learned friend suggests I arrange the letters cross-wise.

```
            P
            A
            T
            E
            R
PATERNOSTER
            O
            S
            T
            E
            R
```

which is powerful principally because it reads in most directions, but means (if anything) that Arepo the ploughman holds fast the wheels, which was his job. "Good for him", I think.

Hard by is the crypt of San Lorenzo with tombs from the fifth to the twelfth century. Do I see the tomb of a pilgrim who struggled bravely over the great St. Bernard and reached the warmth and safety of Aosta only to die of exhaustion? I do, and I'll see many more no doubt.

As I leave by the gate of San Orso, I reflect that, had it been the year 960 and I a merchant, I would have had to pay a tax imposed by the Bishop Gezone on any animals with me 'including monkeys', 'quamvis ridiculosum animal' (even though it is an animal of no value).

I pay a courtesy visit to the Roman Bridge which has been excused traffic-duties on account of extreme old age, and now sits isolated from the modern road by which I set off past the railway sidings, past hypermarkets and furniture salerooms, glass-fronted and groaning with kitsch lampshades and expensive ornaments.

My inner compass and the sun tell me that I am walking eastwards and my map confrms that I must do so for a while if I am to find the route to the South.

I have to loosen my jacket in the warm spring sun, and, in the forecourt of a modern antiques store, the customers are complaining of the lack of rain. I am in the vale of the Dora Baltea, where the scenery matches the poetry of the names. On either side of the river stand castles etched against the skyline. Fenis, Cly and Quart eye each other malevolently across the valley.

I do not warm to these signs of the domination of local warlords. Their owners ruled through being more savage than those they had subdued. They were brutal thugs, safe behind their ugly castle walls. What is it that makes people lose all critical judgment and sense of history when they see a castle?

Local peasants cowered as they passed the lairs of these petty despots. Merchants and pilgrims paid their dues, and felt safe at least from lesser thieves.

There. I've had my say. It occurs to me also that I have a very bad stitch high up on my right side. I'd better take another dose of pain-killers.

The churches are my resting places, not only to recite the hours but also for a sight of the reliquaries so popular with pilgrims, *Ex votos* in the shape of silver hearts, or eyes or limbs, in thanksgiving for cures. The valley here is steep, and I cross the Dora Baltea on a bridge, knowing I am being narrowed into the same path the pilgrims took.

The Castles of Quart, and the more impressive Fenis note my passing. Cly, hard over the town of Chambave, does not open its gates, but hides its little Romanesque church from me as, no doubt, it did from most pilgrims.

This is a busy international road, a working road. At St. Marcel they boast of the quarries which supplied Vercelli with millstones for its grain. Interdependence brought prosperity to those living on the route.

Chatillon will have to be my stopping point for today. It is now an unattractive modern spa. Here, then, on the road in front of the church I set down five stones as a marker, to remind me of the exact place on the road I have reached, and to give a starting-point for tomorrow's journey.

Wednesday 14th March. To fulfil a vow, it is necessary to keep it to the letter. Beware of those who call on the spirit of the law; they are hiding something. And so I shall keep my vow to walk from the southern slopes of the great St. Bernard down to the heel of Italy using the pilgrim routes. But because I have to return to the Hospital in Aosta, I cannot keep to my original plan which was to lodge each night in a place further south on the route. Now I shall sometimes have to set a marker, return by train to base, and next day begin once more where I left off.

I must also accept that for the time being I cannot do more than 20 miles. a day which is not serious walking, but may make for a good pilgrimage. Indeed, I may be persuaded to revise things downwards. And so this morning I stand in last night's footsteps, reach down and pocket the five smooth stones, and set off for the village of St. Vincent. A local citizen helps me to find a segment of Roman Road cut into the rock itself. It is a touching point. Moved by my interest he leads me back to the remains of a Roman bridge.

Now to Verres, dominated by a castle, which tries to outstare its rival at Issogne. I am drawn to the little roadside chapel of St. Roch.

He greets me in fresco form, with his large pilgrim hat, his cloak, his staff, his dog which offers him a roll of bread. He draws attention to a sore, high on his right thigh (a symptom of the dreaded bubonic plague).

I had no idea how popular St. Roch was. On this route he has several advantages over other popular saints.

1. He actually existed.
2. He walked this road as a pilgrim.
3. He was a genuinely kind man who helped the victims of a fourteenth-century plague, then caught it from them and died.

Daintily he raises the hem of his skirt to show a puss-infected boil, though mercifully he does not expose to us the classic symptoms of the bubonic plaque.

Here once stood hospices for travellers preparing to cross from Burgundy to Italy. Up to the nineteenth century this was a fortified military post. At Bard tolls were taken, though technically pilgrims were exempt. Sigeric called it 'Publei' 'the house where publicans exact their tolls'. Nowadays there is no sign of a border, and I reflect on the ease of modern travel. Medieval pilgrims, lay or clerical, carried a letter from their Bishop testifying to their *Bona Fides*. Even today a priest carries a *Celebret* ('He may celebrate Mass') and shows it on arrival at a church or monastery. Later, in the time of the Grand Tour, comfortable travellers carried letters from members of the English or Scottish establishment, recommending them to local worthies. With these they also tried to pacify petty officialdom at border posts. In modern times the pilgrim relies on a passport, though the system in England is not as democratic as in other countries, since all poorer classes have to go cap (and brown envelope) in hand to the more comfortable classes, who will then testify to their honesty.

Rapidly to Donnaz, right under the high castle which served so long as a prison, round a sharp craggy corner and onto the very basalt stone base of the Roman road carved out of the living rock and lifting the traveller to safety even should the river become a torrent, and so to Pont Saint Martin, thirty-five miles from Aosta.

Every bridge has its legend, as you shall hear, though Nikulaus of Munkathvera called it "Marteins Kamra" because here was a custom-house on the south side of the border. The medieval hump-backed bridge, remodelled from the Roman, was for centuries the only crossing of the mini-gorge. It leads into the town through a fortified gate, whose first square is named after St. James, of Compostella fame.

I must set myself to find out why St. James is so popular. But here St. Martin is all the rage. He was a fourth-century soldier who was imprisoned as a conscientious objector. We all know that he cut his cloak in half and shared it with a beggar. After becoming a hermit he attracted disciples and began to influence others, becoming Bishop of Tours. In a united Christendom his influence spread as he journeyed into Italy. He took the side of the 'pagan' country areas, and the peasants loved him for it and was one of the first saints who did not have to 'graduate' by being martyred first.

The people desperately needed a bridge, we are told, and the devil offered them one, but at a price: the soul of the first living being to cross it. St. Martin sent a dog over. Exit devil fuming. The same story is told in several Italian towns which have hump-backed bridges at their entrance. Does the devil never learn?

Pont Saint Martin is a comfortable place to stop, for tomorrow I shall allocate myself only the short stage to Ivrea.

Saturday 15th March. A new day and I am walking on the flat. Nothing can be easier. So I have time to explore the church of San Lorenzo, even older than the Romanesque and simpler in style. It is clear from its layout that its baptistery was important. This is the gnarled and tottering ancestor of the high medieval churches. Our Saxon forebears will have worshipped here, when the church was in the flower of its youth and they were on their way to Rome.

I can see Ivrea ahead with the outline of castle and fortified double-towered church merging into one. It is the first Italian city on the road south to Rome. Nevertheless, this was for long the region of the Lombards, against whom history has waged a war of silence, though their name survives in that of Lombardy.

Between the fall of the Roman Empire and the great days of the high middle ages, the Lombards peopled what we patronisingly call the dark ages. These invaders, no more (and no less) brutal than other invaders, carved out dukedoms in both north and south, and borrowed stretches of the consular roads to link them. Their sculpture, full of monsters and tortured humans, is akin to the Celtic, and is considered primitive by lovers of the high Gothic.

I have walked a mere 60 miles but I tell myself, in the words of Dame Julian of Norwich, that at least I have begun, that all shall be well, and all shall be well and all manner of thing shall be well.

The wide plain below Ivrea gives a choice of roads south in the general direction of Rome, and is also crossed by roads going north-west making for the Moncensio Pass and the pilgrim route to Compostella.

But I am one of the Roméi, and so I continue southwards as the Roméi did. When the great days of pilgrimage were ended, the honourable name of Roméo was hijacked by Shakespeare who came across it and liked it. With accent transplanted to the first syllable, it is now synonymous with ill-starred love. Juliet met the boy Roméo. The rest is romantic tragedy

Footling south, I am tempted by the road sign to Piobba ('Public Road'), but to follow the early medieval road would take me unpleasantly close to a motorway, so I take the route favoured by later pilgrims and rest on the east shore of Lake Viveron, a pleasant pond with an undemanding skyline for background.

Today I shall do the afternoon walk to Santhia, a town whose exotic name is only a corruption of Sant'Agnese.

I reach the town centre where stands a solid Romanesque

fortified tower. The church with classic colonnaded porch has an ancient crypt at its heart. Round its inner wall are images of Agatha and Lucy and all the usual band of saints, but sadly St. Catherine's image has been stolen, "Trafugato da ignoti" (spirited away by persons unknown). There is still today a lively trade in stolen pictures, even if the chief suspects are no longer English Milords.

As I come out into the sunlight I see St. Andrew's pub advertising 'Scottish Lagers and Golf Course'. I am drawn towards it; towards, not in.

Between Santhia and Vercelli there is a horribly straight road flanked by a narrow canal. Boredom and unwonted tiredness make me lean on the corrugated crash barrier, and I see two otters frolicking. As I move off, one of them adopts me and half-swimming, half-running, accompanies me for about a mile, then stands up on his hind legs, looks at me and turns back. I pass Cascina di Stra (road-house) and Ca Dé (house of God) which were roadside hospices, but of them remains only the name, and anyway this chain of hotels was reserved, not for Roméi but for Jacobei who were were caught up in the movement, religious and military, to free Spain from the Moor. The name 'Romeo' was assumed as a personal name by those who completed the pilgrimage to Rome, or was handed on to descendants as a family name. I am still thinking of those Jacobei and Roméi as they passed each other on opposite sides of the road.

Vercelli, granary of the north, is in sight, and for the first time since I began this journey I am on familiar territory and I gain from this some sense of security.

I will stay awhile for the sake of St. Andrew whose church was rebuilt with funds from Cambridge. The lunette above the great door shows a crucifixion. Operatic minor characters direct our attention to the central crucified figure, not Christ, but Andrew, who, tradition says, was also crucified. Antélami is one of the truly great sculptors. His art is robust and popular, and as moving today as it was in the eleventh century. This is the earliest Gothic

Church in Italy. The pointed arches inside are supported by flying buttresses outside. I draw a new starting line with my toe in the dust, and go back, as I must, by train to Aosta with only 95 miles of my journey done. I am enduring a third day of the weirdest diet: charcoal, (as unappetising as any neighbour's barbecue), no bread, no pasta, no fruit, no vegetables; though cheese, yoghurt and offal are permitted. I return to Aosta for an echogram, and a decision whether to continue.

I have time to kill in Aosta, window shopping. But there is something nagging me, undermining the simple pleasure of looking at things I do not intend to buy. For two months I have seen mannequin displays spreading from the costly fashion boutiques down to the lower end of the rag trade. Dummies lined up in shop windows. He, all macho and baggy, she in scalloped diaphanous silk, parents and children, including baby, all in camouflage, images of a sad, mindless commercial for war. And now the dummies have taken to the street, and in the churches they dare to come to communion, dressed for war, dressed to kill their fellow humans.

"So this is military chic", I said
"Tell that to the Iraqi dead.
You make me sick".

Thursday 20th March. Fasting from yesterday evening, and with a severe headache, I walk to the hospital. I follow directions given me at the desk, get lost, and find myself lying on a table, watching a live show of a journey through my own kidneys. Yes, I have several microliths near the right kidney: bad news, since it is my left which has had a name for laziness over the last forty years. I do not need the right one to be blocked.

Now they give me a lovely pull-out series of photo-souvenirs of the kidneys and Dr. Monica says, "Keep this on you at all times; It saves time, they'll know what you've collapsed from," I take this as encouragement to continue, and without giving anyone a chance to have second thoughts, pick up a prescription at the desk, thank everyone in sight, and go to buy a ticket for the first train tomorrow to Vercelli.

Friday 21st March. At Vercelli I step off the train and hurry across the station square, stand beneath the great door of the abbey, look up and nod to St. Andrew looking down at me from his cross. Is that an encouraging wink he gives me?

Pavia is 45 miles away. It should be less, but this is rice country and drainage canals, criss-crossing, do not allow a straight route. When was rice first cultivated here? 'Da sempre' (It always has been), say the locals. But I wonder which lucky pilgrims were the first to come home with tales of risottos. On occasion I have seen the flooded paddy-fields shimmering in the distance and wondered why the people have, in such a place succumbed to the demands of tourists, and allowed the local economy to be threatened by the Neapolitan Pizza.

This broad plain has seen countless battles. One of these in 1859 was more bloody than most and has a tower monument praising the dead who gave their lives against the Austrians at Palestro.

In earlier times, Palestro had its "Domus Infirmorum" (House of the Sick), the ancestor of our infirmaries. This shelter for the weaker pilgrims was provided by the Hospitalers of Sant'Antonio di Vienne. There is a scattering of churches all along the road, some, as at Robbio, abandoned and half-heartedly restored, others like St. Peter's have had to be rescued from over enthusiastic nineteenth-century restoration. They feature in the old chronicles. Philippe-Auguste stopped at Roable (Robbio) in 1191 on his way back from the third crusade. Now these buildings show their scars to attract the pilgrim's pity.

On this long and easy stretch I have stopped at times to dip into the *Chansons de Geste* (songs of the deeds of the bold knights). They speak of the eighth and ninth centuries but were written in the eleventh and elaborated in the thirteenth centuries. They were promoted by the Monks of Cluny: the military and the monks had a common interest in the Holy Land. Pilgrimage was not just an act of piety it was an assertion of a right to enjoy the Holy Land.

"Le Gente che vanno al servigio dell'Altissimo" (The People who travel in the service of the Most High) were soldiers of Christ. St. Francis, supreme pacifist, spoke of his followers as Knights of the Round Table. The pilgrim, however poor a soldier, wore his badge with pride. As the modern football fan might wear a replica shirt and dream his dreams, so the pilgrim might declare himself ready, to shed his blood for Christ, to die for his faith, as did the heroes of Roncisvalle. Indeed, he might proudly sing of the knights who were dashing heroes vanquishing the Muslims, whom they all viewed as agents of the devil, and a menace to civilisation. These songs were linked to the war in Spain whose aim was to chase every Muslim from Europe. Whereas in Spain for centuries Christians and Muslims and Jews had shared whole cities peacefully to the point where Mosque and church might share a party wall, there came a time when Christians decided to wage a Holy War on the infidel. In the eleventh century, the cult of St. James was invented, and it was in Mortara that I heard of an image at the shrine of Compostella showing St. James slaughtering Moors "Santiago Mattamoros". The *Chansons* were war propaganda. The great pilgrimage to the end of the earth, Finisterre, often undertaken to expiate sin, was part of the movement to cleanse Christendom. The *Chansons* describe battles which took place in Spain and France but use large licence to transfer events to Italy, describing Charlemagne's battles against the Lombards. Saracens appear, angels intervene, acts of chivalry and derring-do take place all along the *Via Francígena*. Here in Mortara they speak in hushed tones of Ami and Amile who died fighting against Desiderius the Lombard in 773. Their bodies were buried in separate graves, only to be found later, together in death in one grave.

Sunday 23rd March. There are worse places than Mortara to stay in, as the pilgrims were aware. Santa Croce is modelled on the

Church of the Holy Sepulchre in Jerusalem, and the Abbey of St. Albino had a cloister offering them minimal shelter. Pilgrims had by now noticed that they were called 'Itinerants'. Then, as now, this could be a term of abuse.

'Iter', a journey, can refer both to a pilgrimage and a military expedition, and the two were often mixed, as was the travelling company. Boosted by military talk there were even naïve pilgrims who believed they could take Jerusalem without striking a blow, because it was the will of God. Virtual reality is not a recent invention; neither is fanaticism. Passing through Tromello, I link it with the Tremel of Sigeric. I have got used to reading his itinerary backwards, and the thought darts that I ought to do at least one stretch of the road as he did his journey, making north, instead of constantly meeting him like this coming towards me.

When I set out from Mortara I had allowed the whole day for this stretch, but I have gone too slowly and there is no twilight. It is suddenly too dark for comfort. For six kilometres the roads take no account of pedestrians, nor do the cars. Breathing in the fumes of homeward-bound traffic I set my sights on the unbeautiful outline of the large Cathedral of Pavia.

I could make for my hotel near the railway station, but decide to seek the line of the pilgrim road which brings me to the banks of the river Ticino, where I can view the pitiful remains of the Roman and medieval bridge. This was not directly bombed in the last war but, in 1947, suffering from post-traumatic stress, it gently subsided into the river. A short distance upstream there stands a twentieth-century reconstruction of a medieval covered bridge, looking very much like a twentieth-century reconstruction of a medieval covered bridge.

And so I cross the river, and avoid looking too closely at the cupola of the nineteenth-century cathedral, one of several claiming to be the third largest in Italy. A claim to be the ugliest would be undisputed.

I go on to the church of San Michele, which is approached by a narrow street but now has an open square in front. The pilgrim would have viewed it from very close, and looked up as at a sandstone cliff. The figures of monsters, angels and symbolic characters now seem to be embedded in it like fossils in a Dorset cliff-face. It was the warrior Lombards who introduced devotion to St Michael in the north of Italy.

Inside and out there are sculptures to frighten and to reassure: an *Annunciation* which is Byzantine yet in high relief. An eleventh-century wooden image of Christ, clad in gold, stares ahead from the cross, and is immensely moving, but it is the plaster statue of Mary facing it that attracts all the candles and petitions. Pavia saw kingly and imperial coronations. When it was not being sacked it prospered well enough. But I am tired and I have a long journey ahead of me tomorrow.

Monday 24th March. This morning I must see the city once more, before making for the River Po. San Pietro, mentioned by Dante, claims to hold the body of the fifth-century St. Augustine, and his Gothic tomb is magnificent; it also has the tomb of Boethius, the philosopher, who died because he was too honest for the Emperor Theodoric (524). Several of the churches served as hospices, and we know of the arrangement by which people slept on straw and received gruel for sustenance.

Through the prosperous suburbs the road leads towards the great river. The hamlet of Belgioioso lives up to its name, for the proprietor of the local food-store greets me as every traveller would wish, and for the money I offer him for cheese, bread and water, to show his total honesty he gives me two receipts, one official (*ufficiale*), he says, the other out of courtesy (*ufficioso*).

The road skirts the river, but at a distance, since the area is subject to flooding. At intervals, I enter the well-kept churches and, as I recite the hours, comfortable women come in to light candles before numerous statues.

Sigeric must have been at ease here as he sauntered northwards, his journey all but completed. He never rushed, and here his road was overlooked by castles and monasteries. He chose Chingolo Po for a resting place and now it has the aspect of a domesticated castle. I choose to follow a sign to a Benedictine monastery, but I am not so lucky. The solid pile is barred and bolted against all but the members of some arcane society. In this lush valley even the dogs are pacifist, a different breed from the suburban hell-hounds of Pavia who this morning hurled themselves at me for daring to pass on foot near their garden wall. I am keeping a record of their verbal assaults.

At Corteleone, whilst aligning my five smooth stones to mark tomorrow's starting point, I know that I must turn due south and seek the ferry they have told me about. The alternative is to go far to the east and cross over to Piacenza by a modern bridge, which would be unsatisfactory, because the pilgrims were ferried across the river Po at this point by boat.

Tuesday 25th March. It is my eleventh day of walking, and now I must make for the 'Transitum Padi' (crossing of the Po).

From prehistoric times until recently, the river created treacherous marshes. Now the road is easy and, where necessary, runs on a raised embankment.

All around the land is rich and fertile and Baronial castles are signposted. Without deviation I make for the river, stopping only to read the excellent information boards which proudly record that Sigeric passed through here and called this stage, the fortieth from Rome, "S. Andrea ad Caudam" (St Andrew on the river-bend). Forty days of walking should also get me to Rome. On the river bank, going through an arched gate, I find myself in a fortified farmstead. Some houses and barns are in ruins, others are comfortably appointed. In the central open space stands a little church. Through the large key-hole, I can see reliquaries glinting on the altar.

At the café by the town gate, I ask anxiously if the ferry is running. "We'll phone the ferryman," say the welcoming women, while two men sit quietly sipping wine at a table nearby. "Yes, he'll be here in less than an hour. He doesn't usually start till May or June, but he'll come for you". So I thank them and go outside. On the bank of the Po where the water has cut into the soft earth and made a steep and crumbling cliff, I sit and sing a verse or two of "The Waters of Tyne".

"O where is the boatman to carry me o'er?"

Here he is, coming from a mile downstream, but how to get down to the boat? Since autumn's last crossing, the steep iron ladder down to low water has lost several rungs, and my backpack threatens my balance. But with one bound, I am safely aboard. Danilo Paris, may his name be blest (he and the company of ferrymen who know the sacredness of their mission), speaks of the groups of foot pilgrims who do this stretch as we go downstream to Calendasco. Here, this Christopher, who by now knows that I am an English priest, invites me into his rambling, comfortable, welcoming house and introduces me to his wife and tiny baby. By way of hospitality, he offers me food and also wine, which I drink though it is Lent, for certain people there are who have power to countermand a mere human vow. The wine is red and of the local variety, being 'Naturalmente Effervescente'.

In this house, Danilo has welcomed not only pilgrims but also those who have plotted the ancient pilgrim route, Renato Stopani and others of the Society of Roméi. He also mentions the names of those who can help me on my route to Rome. Makers of roads, builders of bridges, ferrymen, these were the saints in the pilgrim's catalogue. St. Christopher, (did his story or his name come first?) a giant of a man who lived by a deep and dangerous ford and saw the people over safely, till one day he carried over a small child and found him almost too heavy, for the child was also carrying all the burdens of the world, being the Christ-child.

Throughout Christendom, any church which welcomes pilgrims (as St. Albans) has a giant St. Christopher painted on the wall. In

Italy, almost all rivers (except in the furthest south) run east – west or west – east, and therefore pose a barrier to the southbound traveller. Portage of some sort is necessary, hence the original meaning of Port, which is the place where people or goods are carried over, which is where St Christopher comes in..

Danilo sets me on my way across the flat land toward Piacenza.

Along the road I come first to San Nicolo – where they are devoted to a saint of Bari, who was originally of Myra in the middle east. His fame was carried back along the road by returning pilgrims.

Here they have also have a pub-restaurant called 'Crocodile-Corner' which is set to welcome Aussies in with gently smiling jaws. There are hospitals ahead of us dedicated to St. Anthony, St. James, St. Mary and St. Lazarus (for lepers). The Templars too had a hospice, San Sepolcro. Irish pilgrims were received at Santa Brigida. But the guests were not all pilgrims; this was the route to France and the Champagne Fairs.

As I enter the bustling city of Piacenza, I find that it is possible to like it a lot, and to regret that it has had to struggle so hard to keep its ancient beauty.

A massive castle, a Gothic Palace, churches of most periods mixed together, museums, and a history which compares with most northern cities. I shall leave soon, only because I need to keep going.

Thursday 27th March. ... But not far, only to Fiorenzuola by the Via Emilia.

Abbot Nikulaus was doing 25 miles a day, on horseback I suppose, though Belloc averaged 20 miles day on foot. First, I must shake off the suburbs of Piacenza, and get to Ponte Nure. Bridges, so easy to identify, have usually been on the same spot for ever. This one has two Roman piers remaining and as I scramble down to the river's edge and get out my camera, a car draws up and in polite Italian Policespeak an armed man asks me why I am photographing a bridge. "Why not?" I think, but decide to answer obliquely. Beginning with Noah's flood and the rainbow, I narrate the history of bridges, (though I do not remember any mention of a bridge in the bible). After a while, I look up: no car, no police.

The village church has tower and apse in russet brick, and stone caryatids. Only the classical porch strikes a jarring note. As I sit opposite with a lemon drink, the police car comes up slowly. They could not resist coming back.

Do you mind if we ask where you come from? "From the Gran San Bernardo", I say, "and on foot". Their awed silence permitting, I pull out a book from my side pocket and give them Sigeric's Stages. Which reminds me that I must be getting on to the next one, Cadeo (*Casa Dei*, House of God) with its little gem of a lunette over the church door, showing Madonna and child.

So to Fiorenzuola (Sigeric called it 'Foricum').

Here Eric Svendsson, 'the Good,' founded a hospice for Scandinavian pilgrims. I could turn aside here and go by the Val D'Arda, past Castel Arquato, reach Val di Taro and so to the Cisa Pass. It is tempting; I have dear friends of many years at Morfasso but I have promised to see them later in the year and share the feast of Santa Franca with them.

My choice is to go to Parma. The reason will soon be clear.

Friday 28th March. The road to Parma is short and easy. I have time to make a diversion on foot, as many pilgrims did, to the Abbey of Chiaravalle. The great St. Bernard of Clairvaux, who founded it, was the inspiration behind the Cistercian order which spread vigorously through Europe in the twelfth century. Though personally likeable he was fierce on principles. The monastery he founded here is a well preserved delight, even down to the entwined columns like sticks of liquorice. In the cloister a notice printed in red on glass reads "SAFE CRASH. TO CRASH IN EVENT OF FIRE". An emergency notice unintelligible to Italians, risible to the English.

The overall memory is of Verona Marble, sandstone and *cipolino* which were only available because the roads to many quarries were open and popular devotion supported the labour of the stonemasons.

The peaceful hamlet is grouped around the monastery, and is surrounded by prosperous fields within sight of the ring-road north of Fidenza.

I have only to step back onto the main road, go under the ring road, and walk into Fidenza, Borgo San Donnino of Medieval times. Many towns on the route owe a big debt to their local saint. Here a declining city was renewed (posthumously) by Donnino, martyr and rescuer of travellers. Today we trust ourselves to travel insurance companies; the medievals turned to St. Christopher, St. Martin or to local saints. Donnino's church is a brilliant shop-front. The Pieve (*Plebs* = people = church) is stunningly decorated. The carving is both popular and high-class, full of prophets. Christians knew their Old Testament and for them it pointed towards the New. The three wise men are there; pilgrims felt a common bond with them.

If the front wall of the church is solemn, then the side is totally human. There the traveller could see pilgrims like themselves, men on horseback, women on foot, all seriously dressed for the journey. At Fidenza many pilgrims leave us for the Monte Bardone, but I shall continue with those who make for Parma, which is also a pilgrim city and once had eighty hospices, some of them free to pilgrims.

Saturday 29th March. The little village of San Pancrazio, or more precisely its church, is an unexpected find. I was simply thinking of getting to Parma but, as no open church door goes unentered, I go in and sit down, vaguely thinking of our own St. Pancras, not the classical church near Euston, but the frail and beautiful Norman survival set in greenery behind St Pancras station. But here, on the pilgrim route to Parma, in the village church they have re-used Corinthian capitals. The lighting is subdued, but enough to read the daily office, from which I am distracted by a name carved into the bench in front of me, 'The Pellegrini Family'. I do not think it is by chance that they have sponsored this bench. Is it a local family wishing to carve their name with pride in memory of a footsore ancestor? Did a foreign pilgrim settle down here and found a family?

We are in the suburbs of Parma with its reputation for comfort, good eating and (which is not the same) good taste. It never disappoints, but today I'm a pilgrim with lodgings fixed, so I make across the city with its many bookshops, markets and competitive food shops.

Red brick can be as beautiful as stone, and a mixture of both can be even more satisfying. Off-loading my backpack I make for every pilgrim's goal, the cathedral and baptistery. These were completed in one of Parma's great periods, the eleventh and twelfth centuries, though the campanile came a century later.

Parma is famed for painting, music and literature. I have to focus my mind on my present pilgrimage. Correggio, Parmigianino, Verdi, Toscanini and all great people who left your mark here, I salute you, but no early pilgrim ever met you. I creep into the great church, and, trying not to appear to hurry, I make for the right transept. There are no doubt many who would be lifted heavenward by the vortex of Correggio's *Assumption of the Virgin* in the dome. I forgo the thrill and turn aside to the carved *Deposition from the Cross*, the only work Antélami certainly signed.

In any age, this sculpture would be remarkable. With a minimum of lines he creates both movement and emotion. In the centre Nicodemus lifts down the dead Christ, whose outstretched right hand embraces the Church of the gentiles, led by Mary. A horizontal angel gives the victory to this side. The left arm of Christ, still attached to the cross, seems to hang in judgement over those on the left, including the gambling soldiers. An angel pushes down the head of a mitred Jew. Antélami, a man of his age, sees the New Testament as triumphing over the Old. If the mood is not sympathetic to the Jews it is far removed from the ghastly anti-semitism of the story of little St. Hugh and paintings I have seen in Catholic churches repeating medieval slander.

The baptistery is on the square. On the outside, it is of sober beauty, but the interior cries out to the pilgrim: "You are part of my story. Look up and recognise the seasons, the labour, the rest, the rewards of hard work." The seasons are accompanied by the signs of the Zodiac, not because the medievals were stupid enough to believe in astrology, but because in those days even town-dwellers could still see the planets at night, and by their conjunctions establish a calendar. In fresco and in stone the major events of salvation are set out. Companion saints, by now familiars, stand around, as though ready to engage in conversation.

As the pilgrim left the baptistery, his last encounter was with the lunette inside the door, carved stonework brightly painted; the flight into Eqypt.

Like St Joseph, the pilgrim dreamt dreams and was compelled by them to travel without comfort or the guarantee of lodgings. His family was viewed with supsicion and treated as itinerants by those they met on the way, but he knew all the while that somehow it was all part of God's plan.

Romanesque carving presupposes a shared experience between the character emerging from the stone and the character looking up at it.

Reluctant to depart, I fix Joseph and Mary and the Angel well in the mind's eye and leave the baptistery at last.

The Cisa Pass

Monday 31st March. This is my last chance to go towards the coast. Foot-pilgrims travelling thus far down the *Via Emilia* did so in order to keep to Lombard territory on a road which led to the dukedoms of the south. The custom continued when the road came under Frankish dominion.

I am expecting good things of the Taro Valley, but my first impression is of heavy lorries on a very straight road, and chain-link fencing protecting a military base from unarmed citizens.

On the edge of Collecchio is a shrine: "Aedes BMV Lauritanae dicata" (The House dedicated to Our Lady of Loreto), a sign of a late devotion to the transient house of Loreto, which has spread with returning pilgrims from the Marche.

The village church was ancient until the restorers had their way with it, but one carving remains of a lively acolyte or Master of Ceremonies in a procession. (Pilgrims loved processions.) The corner café provides food that is fresh and tasty, and I ask the owner about the signs for Parmalat, which, for the first time, I connect with Parma and milk. He explains that the huge company began here in a small way and bought up the local co-operatives and guaranteed them a market, and for this at least they are grateful.

Ahead of me lies a national park where the pilgrim road sought higher ground. Tomorrow's task.

Tuesday 1ˢᵗ April. Walking a route is the only way to understand a map. I was convinced that I was taking a dog-leg eastwards and a roundabout road for historical reasons. Not so; it makes sense to go fairly directly over the mountains to the sea. Given that Italy tilts sharply from n.west to s.east, I'm making almost due south towards Rome.

Now the road winds up into the wooded hillside, not a heavy lorry in sight, and the local people are most willing to point me towards Talignano, set among the trees. Just a church and a row of houses, with people at the door and children playing. Over the church door is a lunette in stone. Unusually for Italy the scene is the weighing of souls on judgement day ('psychostasis'''): Souls in the Scales. Angels push one side upwards, devils drag the other side down. Forget the dynamics or the logic; the message is clear. I've seen the same in Arles, in Provence. Art and sculptors travel.

Down to the Taro again to stop and stay at Fornovo, a market town which was new in Roman times, and still is a nodal point today. They claim that the church of Santa Maria Assunta is the oldest church around. Sigeric would have rested in the open porch of this church before the constant passing traffic generated enough money for the people to call in Antélami to enlarge and modernise it. The altar frontal has scenes from the life and martyrdom of St. Meynard. Something for the pilgrims to talk about at their evening meal.

On the outside wall a pilgrim, headless now, and weather-beaten, carries his 'besace' (bag) and all the traditional bits and bobs. He seems to be very well provided. He needs to be: the Cisa Pass can be lonely and wild, though not at this time of the year.

For once, I must mention the hostelry, run by the Cavalieri family with every modest comfort, good local food and a concern for the traveller. They even agree to store my heavy books, knowing I will come back for them later. I tell myself that I'm right to carry only the essentials over the pass. Benet Biscop left all the book-carrying to his donkey.

How many pilgrims walked the whole way? The rich went on horseback, others used donkeys. The ancient Fathers of the Church decreed that women should not go on pilgrimage at all, because, being weak, they would need lifting onto horse or ass, and this would involve undue physical contact with the men who lifted them onto the animal. Egeria, the fourth-century probably Spanish nun, ignored such chauvinist tosh.

I have time to wander and enjoy the town, and, just for the fun of it, to ford the river, stepping from boulder to rock. So I sit on a large smooth boulder with water lapping around me and think of Sigeric homeward bound and Nikulaus going towards Rome and just missing him by about 170 years.

I'll bide a while here and then tackle the pass. The forecast is for wintry weather. Perhaps that will be a relief; up to now, most days the temperature has reached 25 Celsius.

Wednesday 2nd April. Several people have mentioned two comfortable refuges on the pass, and I jot down the telephone numbers. I'll use one or other according to progress. A zig-zag short-cut gets me to the road I want.

At Sivizzano, the parish priest is away but Pietro Adorni, living in one of the houses on the courtyard alongside the church, invites me in and offers me refreshment. He is delighted to use his conversational English as we share a common interest in Belloc who forged his own way to Rome, though not on this path. Civilised conversation is as good a pick-me-up as any in this out-of-the-way place. "There's nothing worth the wear of winning but laughter and the love of friends", as Belloc himself wrote.

Pietro leads me to the village square, speaking of the hospice which once was there. He points out the right road and bids me godspeed.

Once out of the village, I can see the outline of the squared foundations of buildings which could come from any century, but resemble the remains to be seen along Hadrian's wall. A gentle rain, little more than a mist, begins to fall, and I can make out the villages along the hillside which were once strung along the route. I fish out my mini-umbrella, which looks ridiculous when held above a back-pack, and I'm happy when the rain turns to light fluffy snow. At this point no track can make greater claim than any other to be the original, since pilgrims went higher or lower according to the terrain to keep above the flood plain.

Running along the bottom of the valley is the fine road I have spurned. It was projected, but not completed, by Napoleon.

At Terenzio, a villager sees me looking at their little church and tells me it is 3,000 years old. I try to look suitably impressed, but maybe he means that it was built on top of a pagan temple. My incongruous umbrella has long been folded, but now I can actually feel the weight of the snow on my head and shoulders. Huge wet snowflakes settle on everything. I'm glad they said they would watch out for me in Cassio; it can't be far out of sight.

Out of sight? The track I am on has already disappeared. I think I'd better start making for the bottom of the valley and the state road. The horizon and the more distant trees have vanished, even the trees nearest me are limned in white. I do not know if I am in the middle of a field or on the road.

I must simply keep going downwards – there must be some houses near the state road. I cannot lift my little legs high enough to make progress and if I push through the snow I make a wall in front of me. Everything is suffused in white light. I suppose it is like being inside a cloud. If I didn't know where my feet were, I wouldn't know which way up I was. It is many years since I experienced whiteout (on the lakeland fells). It is scary and dangerous.

Suddenly a gust of wind punches a hole in the wall of white. Below me I can see two snow-ploughs and a tiny ribbon of road which grows as they clear it. No sound; is it a mirage? I shout and wave. How pointless! But now I couldn't care, I'm safe, and although for a while the snow and cloud cover me again, I'm soon below it all and sliding down on mini-drifts to the road which is clear, but empty – except for an elderly man coming out of his cottage (one of a row) to clear his path. At first surprised, he invites me in to take some soup. "Has my car become stuck in the snow?", he asks. "No", I say. "Madonna ! You're not walking?" he cries, and he tells me it is only six kilometres to Cassio.

Looking back at the way I have come, it seems that a stretch of two or three miles has caught most of the snow and stored it. Just my luck to have been in the thick of it. The road is now scraped clear. The weather is tolerable. At Cassio they are looking out for me. Across the narrow, ancient main street they are discussing the sudden change of weather as they clear away the snow. On the wide state road, which slices through the village, stands the refuge.

At the café opposite they set me by the wood fire, and put a meal on the table. Chicken, pasta and wine are served by a sable-bearded man who is the image of Garibaldi, and dressed not unlike him. Courtesy forbids that I mention the resemblance. He is a gentle, civilised man. The owner waits for me to finish then takes me over the road to the Casa Cantoniera which has been adapted as a refuge. When the road was built in the nineteenth century, these large solid square houses were set along it at intervals. In the basement and roof there was storage space. Between these were living quarters for the family which maintained a stretch of the road on either side.

I am given a room in the attic, with a wooden bed. Blankets and sheets are optional extras at a very modest price. The semi-circular windows are at floor level. To take in the dramatic view to north and east I have to lie flat on the wooden floor. The log-fuelled furnace below has killed the frost, so I can dry out my clothes and take a long rest.

Thursday 3rd April. When the Franks ousted the Lombards they still referred to the road system through the valley and the mountain crossing as the "Mons Longobardorum" (The Mountain of the Lombards). It features in the *Chansons de Geste*. Breakfast, served by Garibaldi, is full and generous. As he sits down with friends, I know they are discussing the traveller. They do get regular visitors, but most are motorised and are stopping for a snack. Today the snow-ploughs pass through again, this time going west.

At last, the restaurant owner appears, having promised to sort out passport details. Why was I chomping at the bit? It's only 8.30 a.m. I sign the pilgrims' book, (it has that title), asserting a fellowship with thousands of others who must have looked up at the pass ahead and felt drawn to it. I even splash out on a tiny pilgrim badge and a *Via Francígena* pen.

Berceto is just ahead. Only a covering of ice on the road, but the fields are deep in snow. I stop for a drink and a *focaccia* in a café and from a nearby table a man comes across and asks if I'm the *pellegrino* who came through the snowstorm.

Pay attention: here is the story of S. Rémy

Bishop Moderatus came from Rheims in France carrying Saint

Rémy's relics, but while camping before attempting the pass he hung the relics on the bough of a tree, and forgot them. After a short while he remembered and came back, and reached up to retrieve the precious casket. The branch rose higher, always out of his reach. This he took to be a sign from heaven that the relics were to stay in Berceto. Later the bishop himself came back from France to spend his last years here, putting the town on the map, where it sometimes appears as Moderan. There are worse places to die.

Berceto already had its Monastery of Sant Abbondio founded by the Lombard King Luitprand. The building is comfortably solid and old, and there is a moving crucifixion over the door. Standing in the square before the church I realise people are having to move to go round me. I don't care, this pilgrim is caught up in something bigger than himself.

At Tugo there is another Casa Cantoniera, adapted as a restaurant, over which there are very comfortable rooms. From Cassio they have telephoned ahead and so I am made welcome. This is luxury, with an evening meal added. I regret that I have to make a firm decision not to seek out Corchia which is a short distance to the north with, it is claimed, the best preserved 'zenodochium' (medieval travellers' rest) in Italy. I do not wish to be stranded again, or to be cut off by snow.

Saturday 5th April. The road is so pleasant and the slope so reasonable that it seems almost cheating to find things so easy on the way to the top of the Cisa.

I rarely take photos of myself or ask others to do so, but my thirty- year-old camera has a delay button, and I set it on top of my back-pack, and my pack on the road and I walk on. A car slows down politely so as to keep out of the picture. The pass itself is dramatic enough, with storage space for goods built into the rock on one side, and a little pinnacle on the right, with steps up to the church of St. Nicholas of Tolentino. Picked out in snow it is almost too neat and squeaky clean. I do not know the reason for local devotion to this saint from the far away Marche.

As if a door has closed behind me, I find I have lost the Taro Valley, and now in front of me the tree-clad slopes will lead me to the Val di Magro.

Generally, weather seems to come from the West. But this side of the mountain escaped the worst of the recent weather and what little snow there is, is bathed in wintry sunshine. Once over the top, the natural stopping place is Montelungo. Of this village the main road is the life-line; its side streets are merely the irregular linking spaces between the stone houses. It is half asleep. It is unexciting. It will do. I ask an elderly lady, "When will the village church be open". "Mai", she says sadly, "Never".

So I wander down a level or two for exercise and enjoyment and it is warm enough to sit for a while on a bench and take in the view. Pilgrims didn't have such luxury, they were glad to seek the safety of the Hospice of Santa Maria della Cisa or the protection of the Knights Hospitallers at San Benedetto. The many Orders of knights involved in the crusades placed their houses strategically along the route. All part of the war effort. This was a dangerous spot. The medieval statutes of Pontremoli (the nearest sizeable town) ordered the trees at the side of the road to be cut down to the distance of a cross-bow shot on either side, so that no felon could lurk.

Sunday 6ᵗʰ April. An early start will give me every chance of Sunday Mass on the hoof along the route. That is my thinking, but the descent is steep and for the first time my ankles have become quite sore. Why is it that a descent of a few miles, even on a good road, can strain the ankles as uphill travel seldom does? More worrying is the fact that, though my pack is not too heavy, my back is sore in a way that usually signals kidney stones are on the move. Where is the nearest hospital? Pontremoli, I suppose.

But before I can start to feel too sorry for myself, I arrive at the village of Migneno where the people are gathering for Mass. Freely

I enter with them, and as I sit down my pew-neighbour moves to make space for me and my back-pack.

There is something good about a village Sunday Mass, well celebrated by priest and people. It is so particular that it is universal. And afterwards, there is something good about the local *focacette* bread, chestnut rich, and tasting of the oven. From the square in front of the church, I look back on the road from the pass, down which I have walked. In the foreground are the stone houses lining the stream which runs to meet the Magra River.

Peaceful? Yes, but a carved memorial tells the visitor that this place was burnt down because of the naivety of the local people: "Helvetiis Foedifragis, civibus incautis" (the Swiss were treaty-breakers, the citizens were too trusting). Is the treachery still remembered?

The peaceful normality of this backwater might cause a visitor to forget that once this was a bustling highway. Near Pontremoli Castle stands the sawn-off apse of the very ancient St. George's church once attached to a large hospice. Elsewhere on the wall of a house is a proud little plaque: "Stadino Bonaparte, origin of the dynasty of Napoleon, lived here." There is time enough to enjoy Pontremoli which lies at the meeting-point of the Verde and the Magra Rivers and which, as well as a castle, has several bridges. Over one of these I lean in the evening calm as the swifts dart and dip on the river surface with incredible skill. How is it they never collide?

At a small restaurant it is the menfolk who sit and pick over the day's news. Not a woman in sight. At first I sit alone, but soon their polite curiosity is roused, and when they learn of my journey they begin to discuss the possible routes to Rome. They have only a modest interest in churches, but tell me not to miss the labyrinth in a floor carving in the local church of Saint Peter's. I take note.

When I make to leave and approach the cash desk, the owner at first does not even get up from the convivial table, and then is most reluctant to charge the full amount. We compromise on a very fair price. Honour is satisfied. I had not intended to sing for my supper.

Monday 7ᵗʰ April. I keep thinking of the prehistoric collection I saw yesterday in the castle. I could never have imagined the Villanovan stone sculptures, and now they will not let me rest. Narrow, flat stone pillars, humanoid forms, big eyes and vestigial bodies, which critics once dismissed as primitive art. In the old days not many medieval pilgrims will have come across them. Any who did will have found them abhorrent. Few carvings have survived, partly because Christians regarded them as pagan idols, though the shapes and forms survive in some Lombard and Romanesque art.

This morning I must go south through the town which has 'characteristic', even 'suggestive', streets as the guide books say. At the limit of the old town is the church of St. Peter, disappointingly modern (having been liberated by allied bombing), in concrete glass and brick. But the sandstone floor carving has survived, a circular maze for which pilgrims needed no explanation. It represented the road to Jerusalem, was full of false starts, deviations, blind alleys and every roadside danger. Christians, it seems to me, have taken a Greek myth and given it a new life.

I'm starting late today, and there's heavy cloud, but there is no danger of a snowstorm in this sheltered valley. It is hard to believe that this was once a highway leading to a major junction in Christendom. The winding, shallow Magra River is my only companion. Or is it merely going my way? Not far out from Pontremoli I am walking for once on the right hand side of the road, since there is a narrow footpath, when a car passes and then draws up ahead of me, and out steps Garibaldi. He runs back to me delighted, almost triumphant, this quiet man. He is a part-time builder and decorator and must travel to survive.

I have proved him right, I *was* walking the route, as he can tell his friends, starting with his workmate in the car.

We are standing in the middle of the road, and he clearly must get back to his car, but I cannot resist mentioning Giusepppe Garibaldi, whom he so resembles. "Yes", he says, "A great man, but I have no time for war." "Shake hands", I say, "You're speaking to a pacifist."

The neat little church-complex at Sorano is not even famous, but the tower, apse and façade are as familiar and reassuring as the local branch of a favourite chain-store.

Inside, tucked in a corner, is the prize and goal of my visit, but first I deliberately recite the day's midday prayer and only then reward myself with a close look at the Menhir to which the church has given asylum. Reverentially I touch it, as I was not allowed to touch the ancient stones in the museum back in Pontremoli. If the early Celtic missionaries had had their way, perhaps not even this one would have survived.

I go out into the churchyard which is overhung by a steep hill topped by the battlements of a walled village. Filatteria crowns the hill. Over the centuries it has not so such changed as evolved. It takes little imagination to people the streets with pilgrims who had left the road to seek safety. 'Filatteria' is Greek for watch tower: why were pilgrims who were passing through Lombard or Frankish territory seeking refuge in a Byzantine stronghold? I go through the narrow streets with their pilgrim links, churches and hostels, onwards to where the village loses itself in the well-ploughed fields. Here an eighth-century church, sometime dedicated to St. George, is rooted in the soil It contains a stone which lovingly recalls that the Lombard Bishop Leodgar came to the help of pilgrims. They had grief enough from bandits and from petty local landlords demanding tolls from wayfarers and welcomed protection wherever they could find it. Who, for instance, were the kindly Knights of Tau of Altopascio? Since Parma they have dogged my steps, so that I half expect them to leap out on me from the brushwood, armed cap-à-pie. Though their title now sounds somewhat Monty-Pythonesque, in fact their sign, Tau, is the last letter of the Hebrew alphabet and transcribed as a T-shape it is the true form of Christ's cross. Clearly the knights were very active along the *Francígena*, but their base was in the Arno valley. Perhaps there I shall get explanations.

Villafranca. Names are important. The Franks, we may presume, were here. Through the course of history invading armies left their mark, like dogs on trees. This is yet another little walled village. Its gates have become arches, now open and welcoming, but once they were heavily shuttered and marked the line of customs, control and curfew.

Tuesday 8th April. The river meanders and the modern road keeps me above the flood-plain. I have a vision of the church of St. Mary, isolated in the curve of the river below. To get to it I have to clamber down and find my way through a quarry. Ferocious notices warn of danger, but there are workers below with heavy machinery. Where they can go, so can I. It is sad to see this church, not ruined but abandoned and doubly cut off from the road it once served. As I pick my way back to the road, I can see that the whole area is an open-cast gravel pit. No doubt the excavating company, having made its money, will landscape the lot and make a path down.

On the side of the modern road, to which I have returned, there is a trite and ugly shrine to Our Lady with a ghastly collection of *ex votos*. The need to give thanks for good fortune is very deeply ingrained but here it is not accompanied by the faintest scintilla of artistic taste.

By the roadside, not for the first time, I see a little memorial to policemen. These died in 1940 "in the course of duty".

Aulla marks an important junction with the road from the Garfagnana, which in a great curve would also get me to Lucca through villages I've already visited over the years, but I must stick to the chosen coastal route. Aulla, being strategic, was, of course, bombed in the last war, but a castle and part of a pilgrim church survive.

Sarzana has more to show, both a northern and a southern gate, with a main street in between. There's a sureness and a certainty about such stretches. Here pilgrims walked, though Sarzana gained importance only after Luni declined.

In Roman and medieval times Luni dominated the area and was a major land and sea junction linking Compostella, Rome, the Holy Land and northern Europe. Only the bare bones remain, as we shall see.

Wednesday 9th April. I must walk the length of Sarzana again, ceremonially entering by the Parma gate, through which pilgrims walked over a couple of centuries. This is now a modern comfortable town which does not depend on its past, but has not destroyed its history. On right and left there are small-scale tidy shops, and all you could want in a local centre. On through the Porta Romana and down to Luni, and I'm as eager as any explorer with ruins in his sights. It's not my first visit to to Luni and once again I'm selfishly glad to find it has few visitors. I prefer to take in its emptiness all on my own.

Here are flat fields, typical of a coastline where land and sea have for centuries wrestled for mastery.

The devastation wrought by marauding Saracens and equally savage Normans was given decent burial by the Magra River as it silted up the estuary and Luni disappeared.

Recently private houses, hedged and gated, have been built with no respect for the original town plan. The only relic of any importance is the amphitheatre, which has been well restored behind an ugly chain-link fence. How can anyone give way to nostalgia with nose pressed up against such a barrier ? Today Luni is one of the least-known Roman and medieval towns. There was a time when it was the goal of thousands from the far north bound for Rome or the Holy Land and for people of the south bound for Compostella. Dante, in *Il Paradiso* XXV.17, speaks of "*Il Barone* [St. James] who, down on earth, draws souls to Galicia [Spain]".

From here boats set out and coasted from one safe haven to another along the Ligurian coast, on to Toulouse and thence to Spain. It was here more than anywhere else on the map of Christendom that pilgrim paths crossed. Visitors were hugely impressed by the magnificence of Luni. One Scandinavian came thus far and returned home convinced that he had seen Rome.

I am entirely on my own and here I sit for a while and brood. Then, "Come away", I say, in the words of Tennyson's *The Deserted House*, "for life and thought here no longer dwell; but in a city glorious – a great and distant city - have bought a mansion incorruptible. Would they could have stayed with us." I must stop talking to myself.

Making back to the main road, I stop to chat over a garden hedge with a local resident, who is only vaguely aware that the site is sacred. Nor does she understand why I should want to walk as far as Carrara. At Avenza a suburb of that city I find lodgings and a welcome. I can be comfortable here and take time to explore the famous city a few miles inland at the foot of the hills made of marble. I do not know if pilgrims were interested in the quarries. I fancy not.

I remember years ago being taken by an aged quarry-worker from Vagli Sopra into a small quarry on the far side of the Garfagnana on the opposite slope of the Apuan Alps. The two of us together did not amount to ten foot tall, and we skipped from ledge to ledge, ducked under overhangs, and squeezed round corners on narrow tracks over the sheer drop to the quarry floor. I might be more cautious now. In Carrara the trips are organised and safety-conscious to the point of being tame.

On the straight road to the city up from the coast there is an excellent museum with a brilliant collection of marble, a history of the quarry and every explanation you could want. The Cathedral of St. Andrew suffers by comparison with its great and famous Tuscan rivals, but it dwarfs, and seems to subdue, the congregation at Mass.

There is a small railway station in Avenza which serves Carrara and while I am trying to find out whether I might take a day excursion by train north or south, I find myself in a long slow queue. Surely there is no need for the people behind me to push as they do? Yes there was, as I find out later. The outermost flap of my back-pack is hanging loose. I'm annoyed that I have been caught napping by thieves, but do not envy them their takings: an apple core and some cheese parings carefully wrapped.

Thursday 10ᵗʰ April. Pietrasanta is only 10 miles away. Once there, I shall take a break. For this short journey the kindly family who have made me welcome provide me with food. It is a gracious, almost religious gesture.

I am following the old *Via Aurelia* which took advantage of the narrow strip between the Apuan Alps and the Ligurian sea. Here there is now room for an autostrada and a major railway line linking France to Pisa and Rome. Looking across these busy thoroughfares, I seem to be the only one who is not in a hurry. I can enjoy the places in between and play games with names. Why is there a sign for Querceta Loreto (surely a contradiction?) and another for Mirteto? Was the region once carpeted with woody groves of Oak, Laurel and Myrtle?

I've never heard of Pietrasanta, until now that is. But I've chosen to draw a line here and stop my pilgrimage, to concentrate on the celebrations of Holy Week and Easter, to study art and to be with friends. Approaching Pietrasanta from the north I come to a square outside the original town which is shared by an anaemic anorexic Virgin Mary and a marvellous solid massive carving of oxen dragging marble from the quarry to the local stonemason's yard.

This surprisingly attractive town still works marble and is proud of its iron foundry too. I am brought to a halt by a large notice proclaiming "THE STATUE OF SADDAM WAS MADE IN OUR FOUNDRY". Not being up to date on the progress of the most recent Crusade, I look for a newspaper and see a picture of the tyrant's statue being toppled by means of ropes. Bystanders in Baghdad grin. But here in Pietrasanta, how do they feel? Was it pride or annoyance that prompted the public notice?

The hospitality of the inn outside the gate matches the welcoming air of the town. A good place to return to after I have fulfilled a vow by taking part in a snake festival in the Abruzzi mountains.

First I seek out the Missionaries of Africa. Padre Luigi, a long-standing friend who has every Italian virtue, welcomes me into the community, and at the common table I am introduced to members of the community called Romeo and Dante. Serendipity! The omens are good. The religious community begins the celebration of Holy Week together with the local parish. Give Italians a few palm branches, begin to tell the story of Christ's Passion, and in moments you have a liturgy, a celebration. To their credit they do not know how to be bystanders. Nor do they need a Latin dictionary to tell them that 'celebratio' means a lively, noisy assembly. With their help I am already part of the story, but to be part of the mystery I take a train into the heart of the Abruzzi Mountains to lose myself in the crowd, as Sulmona celebrates the central Christian Mystery with rites which would have been recognised by any educated person in Ovid's time two thousand years ago.

This Roméo is ready for the mountains, and has remembered to pack his pocket version of Dante's *Divine Comedy*, not to study the medieval theology of Purgatory, Hell and Heaven – (I've decided I don't understand it) but because I've gained a lot from dipping into the book on the road. It has been pleasant to read his description of a castle while looking up at it. I am sure he was describing things as he saw them, and I agree with those critics who say he walked at least part of the *Via Francígena*, and went as a pilgrim to Rome in 1300, the year of the Great Jubilee.

By now I have realised that Dante makes all the action of the DIVINA COMMEDIA take place between Wednesday of Holy Week and Wednesday of Easter Week, which is the length of time I shall spend in Sulmona.

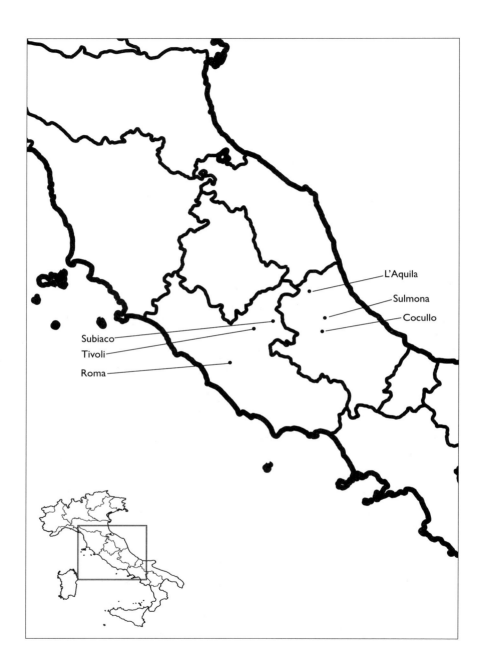

L'Aquila

Sulmona

Cocullo

Subiaco

Tivoli

Roma

Interlude:
Easter, a Snake Festival and Art

Calabria, Puglia, Basilicata were always considered remote and dangerous. But sixty miles East of Rome there is another mountainous region, the Abruzzi, which until the twentieth century, was rarely visited by the travelling classes. The Grand Tour kept to a set route – Venice, Ravenna, Florence, Siena, Rome and Naples. It by-passed the Abruzzi. Then the railways permitted artists and collectors of curiosities to enter the land of the Marsi, the Oscans the Samnites and the Sabine tribes. This whole region, conquered many times by the Romans, was never Romanised.

I remember in the early 1960s watching shepherds from the Abruzzi playing their plaintive strident pipes before the crib in the Piazza Navona in Rome.

I decided then, that I would one day visit Sulmona and the Majella mountains at the first opportunity, and I was just in time to see the last of the 'Pecorai' (nomadic shepherds) as they moved from summer peaks to winter lowland pastures. At that time I took with me the travel books of women such as Estella Canziani and Amy Atkinson, who recorded the sayings and popular poetry of the shepherds and peasants, and, when they could persuade people to sit for them, painted the Albanian women in traditional costume. All this was in the last years of the nineteenth century and the first decades of the twentieth. In the 1970s I was able to get close, but not too close, to the flocks of goat-like sheep, and see the fierce guard dogs mentioned by Amy Atkinson.

Huge white shaggy creatures, that looked as if they had in them parts of bear and wolf. As they rise slowly on the path their eyes gleam red, and their ominous growl sends one's heart into one's mouth.

Times change: the pastures have been turned into ski-slopes, shepherds wear jeans and the women have almost abandoned the wearing of traditional dress, except for great feast days and for times when tourists are looking.

Now, at the beginning of the twenty-first century, I wished to be part of the famous Easter celebrations at Sulmona, where as a climax of the celebrations, a statue of the Madonna is carried quickly through the square ("Madonna che scappa nella piazza"), to greet her son, the Risen Christ.

The region is said to be steeped in superstition, and I looked for the signs, but I did not know how to feel superior to the locals, since I come from a country where vast numbers consult their stars each day and people buy elixirs by credit card. Superstition, folklore and religion: where are the boundaries? In these mountains there has never been a moment when these three were separate.

Stories of saints seamlessly continue the lives and legends of rustic gods. To these people, who have never forfeited the privilege of seeing the sky at night, the stars are familiar. The seasons themselves involve the people in the mystery of death and resurrection. The pagan and the Christian world are not rivals. They live side by side. They need each other.

On Wednesday of Holy Week, I took the train to Sulmona which is ninety miles East of Rome. We followed, for the most part, the *Via Valeria*, the ancient escape-route for those fleeing the pressures of civilisation. From the window I was able to pick out places haunted by those refugees.

At Tivoli, where Cardinal Ippolito D'Este built a costly and grossly pretentious retreat, tourists now wander amongst the famous fountains. The whole town nestles on a cliff and looks across the plain which provides views of distant Rome and of the sun setting behind St. Peter's Dome and descending into the Tyrrhenian Sea.

But look below: there is the Villa of Hadrian, who was one of the good Emperors. He had travelled everywhere, even as far as Scotland, and wished to prepare a bolt-hole for himself, should the cares of state overwhelm him. He built a folly to end all follies, with life-sized copies of every famous place in Greece carved in stone, down to the last detail. He got three years' enjoyment out of it before he died in 138 A.D.

Others fled beyond Tivoli. Horace, who never put his hand to plough or dirtied his sandals, wrote lovingly of his Sabine farm, which he had as a present from Maecenas, the fixer who financed the Empire of Augustus.

How prettily the overweight poet wrote of the romantic toil of the farmer. As my train passed through Vicovaro, I thought of a hot summer's day when I had stood by the fountain of Bandusia, which the poet said was "clearer than cut glass". Here Horace had his villa. This was his escape.

Soon afterwards, but this time to the right, I saw the Monti Simbruini. To these hills Benedict of Nursia fled in the year 500 disgusted with the world. He found a cave below the Lake of Nero (*Sub Laqueo*, which gives the name Subiaco), and though he would have preferred the life of a hermit, he was persuaded to found a monastery, and a movement which, some say, saved European civilisation.

The train next passed the Lucrine Lake, which, from pre-history, was always a malaria-infested swamp. Everyone who was anyone tried to drain it; only in the nineteenth century was the work completed. Now it is an inch-perfect level plain, too vast and too neat to be beautiful, or even to be real. It is the home of the Italian Space Centre - that's escapism for you.

I knew this was the territory of bears and wolves, but my train was just too late to see them. Early twentieth-century passengers on this line were encouraged to look out for the last survivors.

Now I could see the Majella Mountains straight ahead, and I prepared to get out at Sulmona station, a mile outside the town.

Here it was that, in 1943, Red Cross parcels were delivered for the British Soldiers imprisoned in the flatlands two miles outside Sulmona. But I walked freely into the gated town, ignoring the large modern hotel which takes the strain off the three modest Pensiones within the walls. The Hotel Italia, were I've been made welcome for more than thirty years, doesn't offer an American breakfast or any meal at all, except when the family might invite a visitor to join them at their own table. So now I sat down for a coffee and explained that I wished to take part in every event and I was likely to be out at all times of night and day. But first I wanted to question them about their local hero, Ovid. He's reckoned to be one of the great poets, mainly for his *Metamorphoses*, which are stories of the underworld, and every kind of transformation – death to life.

But they spoke only of "Il Gran Maggio Ovidio". Yes, I'd forgotten that Sulmona's greatest citizen was famous for his magic. They speak of sacks of gold buried by Ovid under the roots of trees. There are incantations and tricks which are guaranteed to find the treasure. All this is superstition of course, but so are fail safe methods for winning the National Lottery.

I thanked them for the coffee and *Amaretti*, and went out through the grand front door (this was once a substantial town-house). I went across the little square, down a side street where people sat at tables in the shade, and entered the Piazza Ovidio.

I looked up at the statue of the great man. He was standing on a book of his own poems. Is it open at the *Ars Amatoria* or at the *Tistia ex Ponto*, one of the saddest books ever written.

Beyond the statue is the Art-Deco glass-fronted café which has been a focal point of tourist life since the first English visitors patronised it. The main street, Corso Ovidio, has many a shop which sells confetti – no, not the paper rubbish thrown at English weddings, but true confections of sugared almonds. Sulmona claims that Italian Confetti originated here. They may be right, but the custom of showering married couples with rice or almonds or any other sign of fertility is so old it cannot be dated.

I wish to celebrate Easter. England had its Mystery Plays; Sulmona, under Spanish Neapolitan influence, developed the drama of the Passion in the form of stylised processions with citizen participation.

I need to slow down, to wipe the slate clean, so I walk out of the town over a stream and cross the plain which sixty years ago was the site of the POW camp where British soldiers were held. Among them was a friend, David, who never got to walk the civilized streets of Sulmona or to climb up to Sant Onofrio, the hermitage which was visible from the camp.

I took the steepest route possible, shunning tarmac, to seek it out. Here lived a famous hermit, Pietro di Morrone. He inspired many others and was involved in the thirteenth-century movements which claimed that the age of the spirit had begun and the end of the world was nigh. He became tired, even of these excitements, and wished finally to be alone, but he was well aware that Christianity was in crisis. There was no pope and the cardinals, less than a dozen of them, were making no progress either in Rome, or later in Perugia, in electing a new pope.

Since, even in his positively last retirement the hermit, Pietro di Morrone, often had visitors, he had not been too surprised when one day he saw a mule train, richly caparisoned coming up the track, and in his rock-hewn cell he had entertained Charles II of Anjou, overlord of Naples and Sicily, who asked the respected hermit to write to the dilatory cardinals enjoining haste for the sake of Christendom and the salvation of their own souls. But he may have been surprised at the result, which was another embassy, this time clerical, coming up the track with the news that he, Pietro, was the cardinals' choice for pope. He had had no useful experience, at a time when Machiavelli himself would have been wise to refuse the post.

Pietro accepted and became Pope Celestine V. Being holy, he was a spectacular failure, and within a few months he was persuaded to resign. Dante speaks of "Il gran Rifiuto" (The great refusal) and some think he is condemning Pietro to Hell for his cowardice. I don't think so.

By now I could see pilgrims above me arriving at the hermitage by a different route. Some have come by car. All sought healing of some sort. We go into the shrine and together we descended through corridors and chapels with their ornate little altars, candles and *ex votos* and frescoes. Deep down in Pietro's cave believers rubbed the walls with various parts of their bodies. Discreet questioning revealed that they were suffering from arthritis. They queued to lie down in turn where the saint had rested. They moistened their fingers in the water which ran down the walls and they signed themselves. They seemed to know the rules which are older than Christianity. I sensed the link with the prehistoric pagans and romans struggling up from the temple whose ruins are visible below. For there never was a time when healing was not sought here. And it was to this spot that ex-Pope Celestine tried to make his way to retire for good and all. But Boniface VIII, his formidable successor, could not allow Pietro to become a figurehead for wild enthusiasts (a loose cannon before they had been invented). So he put Pietro in a castle near Naples, for his own good. He died there in 1296.

Going out and sitting on the ledge, I tried to capture the world of Celestine and Boniface. The first naively thought that the dreadful struggle between Church and State would be resolved by some divine intervention. The second bravely took on emperors and kings and was the unsuccessful ultimate medieval pope, as well as being the last.

Dante places Boniface in Hell, perhaps in revenge for his own traumatic experience of exile at the hands of a Florentine faction who had that pope's blessing. But Dante clearly admired the pope's courage and his dignified mien when, almost at the last, surrounded by his enemies who had broken into his palace at Anagni, Boniface endured the insult of Guillaume de Nogaret who belted him across the face with an iron glove. Christ's regent had been slighted. He returned to Rome to die.

"But this will not do." I said to myself "I came here to get away from worldly cares and here am I in emotional turmoil over events of seven hundred years ago!"

So I eased myself down over the rough-hewn steps cut into the rock, knees creaking, since I had not walked much in recent days. Down into the plain through the ruins of temples where many a pagan *ex voto* has been found. I took note of the Christian church built over them, now in its turn a ruin.

The road back to Sulmona passes a vast modern prison with armed guards, barbed wire and turrets. I went through a gate into the city where the streets are lined with opportunistic stalls selling animaloid helium balloons. The shops display jewellery, some of which approximates to the Albanian charms and trinkets which Estella Canziani, early in the twentieth century, painstakingly sketched when, with her father, she travelled through the Abruzzi collecting folklore, choosing peasants to paint and recording styles of dress which differed from village to village. There were others too…

They sensed perhaps that many customs would die out, which is what happened. True, at more remote Scanno, I have seen aged women in traditional dress at Sunday Mass. But I doubt if any will remain in twenty years' time, except in museums and at folksy festivals.

Now, once more, I've reached the square on which the poet Ovid looks severely down. His statue is a copy, I am told of the one near Tomis on the Black Sea, where he died in exile.

He first wrote the Art of Love, and for a time was everyone's favourite poet. The emperor, a humourless man, found the work offensive and dangerous and banished Ovid to the Black Sea.

It is rumoured that Ovid was also close to one or other of the women of the imperial household, and so for a 'carmen et error' (a poem and a blunder) he lost everything. Woe to court poets who offended the emperor. His Tristia ex Ponto in a collection of tear–soaked letters begging for imperial forgiveness and for a return to society life. Never did anyone ever feel so sorry for himself and put it in verse.

If he might not return to Rome then at least might he be allowed to return to Sulmona in it's valley "Crossed by crystal streams, green with luxuriant herbage." His best work, the *Metamorphoses*, is difficult reading now as it is so stylised, stories of gods and goddesses who die and rise again or who are in some way transformed. Does he knowingly wave and nod each year at the procession as it passes by?

Now I felt that the traveller in me must settle down, and let the Easter *Triduum* (three days) take over.

First, I went down into the cathedral crypt where slim columns divide the dimly-lit space. I had an appointment with a favourite sculpture of the Madonna, which is Byzantine in style but almost three dimensional. This simple carving is hauntingly beautiful and deeply spiritual and therefore has no local cult or popular following and remains on a dark and prayerful wall.

Now in the upper church the great mysteries began. The bishop blesses the oils pressed from local olives, but perfumed to show that they are precious and life-changing. They were carried among the people to release healing forces among the community. In the evening, I went to "Santa Maria della Tomba", what a strange title, I thought. What widowed mother, bereft of her son, would glory in the title 'Mrs. Gravestone' ?

There is a Neapolitan tradition of heavy emphasis on, (nay, delight in,) suffering and death. The dignity of the Mass of the

Statue of St Roch

Roman Road at Donatz

Via Francigena

Transitum Padi

The Crossing of the Po

Sculpture of Pilgrims at Fidenza

At the Cisa Pass

Road to Pietro di Morrone's Hermitage

Funeral Procession of Christ

La Madonna che Scappa in Piazza

Snake at Cucullo

Fresco of Pilgrims

Last Supper was ensured by a nun who kept the altar servers firmly under control. To be there in the crowd and not at the altar was for me to be part of the mystery in a different way. But in the best lay tradition I was distracted, because I could see posters on the wall and other signs of preparations for the great events to come. Statues were already in place on their starting blocks. Confraternities had made their plans, statue-bearers had been chosen by competition. As we left the church, friends discussed the vantage points they had chosen for Good Friday and Easter Sunday.

First, on Good Friday the solemn reading of the Passion, one of the simplest ceremonies of the Christian year. The packed churches showed that the people were not just here for the pageantry of outdoor processions. Christ's story is their story, and they were there to hear it

We left Santa Maria della Tomba and stood in the square outside. The prone figure of the dead Christ was carried to solemn music through one square and along the main street of the town.

At 7.30 p.m. huge crowds gathered on the steps of the Annunziata and, as darkness fell, the corpse of Christ was carried on a bier through the narrow streets of the old town. As we set out I was concerned that I was one of only twenty followers, but every balcony had watchers, and most houses had set up shrines: the passing of Christ is a blessing. Back to the main street where the crowd now followed towards the cathedral. The bearers were a confraternity dressed in purple silk. They marched in unique fashion called the 'Struscio' (scuffing) which is defined as 'Strofinare lento e ritmico delle suole delle scarpe a terra'(a slow and rhythmic scuffing of the ground with the soles of your feet).

So, the slow, almost lugubrious, rhythm of the funeral march was emphasised by the scuffing of shoes on the volcanic paving. The people had left the cafés and most showed solidarity with the sacred action. The whole town was in mourning. As we approached the cathedral, I stepped out of line for once and took a photograph. Behind the dead Christ laid on a bier, Mary follows in widow's weeds, all this against the background of the *Pizzeria le Metamorphosi*.

We circled back to a chapel on the main street now decked out as a 'Cappella Ardente' (A chapel ablaze with candles). Christ lay, raised up on high, with the statue of his mother looking down on him. Candles and flowers all around. The people circled the bier and they gave each other rendez-vous for Sunday. They must know the plot.

On Holy Saturday, nothing happens all day – it is a 'dies non', but late in the evening I chose the simpler of the Vigil Masses at San Filippo in the corner of the vast square. There, on the steps of the Church, the priest welcomed the black draped Madonna, as a parish priest would greet a mother who has lost her son. Then the Vigil began, at first subdued. But life and hope cannot be kept in chains for long. Soon the people's profession of faith was followed by the baptism of a child (there are not many adult baptisms here) and all the people seemed to be renewed in that moment. Spontaneously these people shared their joy with strangers such as myself. Mary was given shelter for the night behind the locked doors of San Filippo. As we came out into the vast cold square with its aqueduct and its fountain and its mountain backdrop, it is good to know that death was not the end. But for these people, something of the ceremony of life yet remained to be celebrated.

Those of us who went to Easter Sunday Mass, at Santa Maria Della Tomba, forfeited the best places for the famous event, "Madonna che scappa nella Piazza." But from the church we did send the statues of St. Peter and St. John on their way to rouse Mary and give her the good news.

Everyone knew what must happen next. Peter and John hurried in procession, the crowd making way for them. They crossed one square, under the aqueduct across the whole length of another square, and up the steps to the great church door, where St. Peter knocked loudly. The crowd, always in on the act, knew that Mary would not believe Peter.

By long tradition then John knocks on the door, and Mary is persuaded at last to come out. Still in mourning, she is hesitantly carried across the crowded space. Behind our backs a statue of the Risen Christ has been set up against the solid stones of the aqueduct.

Slowly Mary approaches. Halfway across, she sees her son.

The bearers pick up pace, and soon are running. The black cloak lifts and flies away, doves hidden beneath escape into the crisp spring air. She is dressed in brightest green, symbol of Spring and of Life. Cheers break out. The crowd swirls and turns to follow her and greet the Risen Christ.

Am I a bystander, witness or participant? I look first to the East where the snow-covered slopes of the Majella mountains reflect the sun, but their brightness is rivalled by the unfeigned joy on the faces of this Easter People.

Cocullo and the snake festival

Not far from Sulmona, but off the beaten track, is the village of Cocullo. Even in its national park setting it is rather nondescript. It has no history, but it has a prehistory, and the 'Festa dei Serpari' (Festival of the snake-gatherers), most pagan of Christian Festivals.

At Koukoulion the Marsi worshipped a snake-goddess with rites of spring, featuring snakes at their most dangerous, just waking up full of poison and of pain, till they could find some animal to bite.

That is why I made for Cocullo and stepped mid-morning from a train at the station-halt not far from that village. Others who had come by car were obliged to use the distant motorway for parking and then walk in. The crowds converged on Cocullo, which was well prepared to meet us, stalls set out for the annual day of glory. Locals persuaded visitors to accept a snake, so I did.

I was keen to seek out the Christian element of the celebration, and so I went first to the two churches at either end of the town. These were already full, and there was noise, but a certain intensity of feeling, as visitors sought out their favourite statues and renewed a lively acquaintance with them. At the top of the town where Mass would be celebrated, most seats were already taken, but there was movement, and I followed the stream of people who were going left of the altar to the door in the base of the tower. They knelt in turn to grip a bell-rope tightly in their teeth, so that they would be safe from dental illness for one year more. Some scooped the soil before them, to spread it later, I was told, on their fields.

Mass began, celebrated by a cardinal and a couple of bishops, but it seemed somehow secondary to the constant procession turning left to the tower, and to the honour being paid to the statue of San Domenico. He was the saint who inherited the role of snake-tamer.

Born in Foligno, Umbria, in 950, he was of the Benedictine tradition. Having founded monasteries he always moved on, preferring to live as a hermit. Wherever he went, cures happened; no wonder the people of Cocullo tried to keep him, but he gave them a mule shoe and one of his own teeth as specifics against dog-bites and hydrophobia, against snake-bites and toothache, and he left them.

The tooth in a glass case stood in a place of honour in the church.

Towards the end of Mass tension increased. The statue of San Domenico was draped with large but dopey snakes. I slipped out and edged around the crowd. No chance of a prime spot now. Every corner of every street was crowded, every window, every balcony full.

There were plenty of snakes being handed out, and mine began to take a shine to me, first wrapping himself around my right forearm, and then seeking refuge in my side pocket. He did get an airing once or twice later.

Estelle Canziani writing in the 1920's said the main feast was celebrated in August and she spoke of snakes being thrown hoop-la fashion in the hope that they would attach themselves to the statue and bring good luck. At that time it was considered bad luck if the snake attached itself to the head or halo of the statue. Today I was told that people are discouraged from throwing snakes, though I saw some half-hearted attempts.

One man told me that it brought good fortune to land a snake on the neck or arms of "San Domé" as he called the saint familiarly. "Traditions can vary", I thought.

I was in the crowd, but I was people-watching. Some of them were totally taken up in the passing of the statue, immersed in a magical experience. And there was enough of a spectacle to hold everyone. Before the statue maidens in traditional dress carried bread and fruits of the earth.

The saint must visit every street, every nook; while every cranny seemed to cry out for the totem's blessing.

Not all visitors over the centuries have been peasants. In 1823, Cardinal Della Cenga came here to seek healing after being bitten by a snake. He recovered well enough to become Pope Leo XII.

The procession/visitation now gave way to a secular festival. There were stalls for religious souvenirs, but also stalls offering every kind of junk, stalls providing food for celebration, and stalls making well-earned, much-needed income for locals.

But it was time to leave, I felt, as a small exodus began towards the station. "Back to the very different world of elsewhere", I thought, and then remembered just in time that I was not alone. So, just before the station I pulled from my pocket a reluctant snake, cupped him in both hands, while with his tail he clung to me. I went a few steps up the hill, said a quick goodbye, and the rocks and the scrub took him from my sight.

Art and friends for company

So, having cut short my journey at Pietrasanta, to make a personal journey into Easter, and having participated in a Christo-pagan snake rite, I now sought the company of those who share a love of thirteenth- to fifteenth-century Italian art.

To do this is to saunter and is part of my pilgrimage. *Siragusa Tours* each year takes groups to Padua, Florence and Siena, to study art such as you saw on BBC2, Open University. Here, on site, the tutors impart the knowledge, without seeming to. The participants mix seriousness with the simple pleasures of eating, drinking and sightseeing in good company.

I've never heard the ancient pilgrims making any reference to works of art. I doubt if they were allowed near them. Giotto's moving storied pictures of the life of Christ in the Scrovegni Chapel, Padua, were done to assuage the guilt of a usurer and to purchase pardon. They were no business of the unwashed mob. Even now, visitors must pass through a decontamination chamber, and are allowed only fourteen minutes and thirty seconds to devour them as the clock ticks loudly.

In Florence, the best works of Fra Angelico adorn the silent prayerful cells and corridors of the Friars of San Marco.

True, the Franciscans, Dominicans and Augustinians covered the walls of their preaching churches with lively and popular frescoes, but most of the works which the art group saw in the two separate weeks I was with them (those works, that is, which had not been stolen by our ancestors and brought to England) were commissioned by the rich for their own enjoyment and devotion.

In Siena there is an exception, the Maestà of Duccio di Buoninsegna.

The city wanted the very best adornment for the high altar of the cathedral. Duccio obliged with a majestic Virgin enthroned, surrounded by haloed saints, not quite static, one step removed from the Byzantine. On the back of this painting he portrayed the life, death and resurrection of Christ, picture by picture. All this was to belong to the people. When it was nearly completed, the news spread through the city, and on the day of its transfer the huge two-sided miracle of art was raised high and carried in triumph through the streets to be the focal point of celebration, and devotion not unmixed with civic pride.

It was later removed from the cathedral and is now preserved in aspic. I do not know if pilgrims protested. In general, pilgrims and art do not mix. A good rule of thumb for popularity in religious art is that the more powerfully miraculous an image is, the more ugly it is likely to be. There are very few exceptions and they prove (try and test) the rule.

When the Sienese were victorious in 1260 over the Florentines at Monteaperti, they paid their vows to the Madonna delle Grazie in their own cathedral.

Then in 1661 Cardinal Fabio Chigi built in the right transept a chapel to house the miraculous image. It glows with lapis lazuli and gold and is always full of silent votaries. But come away, step back into the cathedral and the whole of the nearest wall is hung with the crash-helmets of mad, reckless teenagers (photos attached) who owe their brainless preservation to an indulgent Madonna. To this English pilgrim it seems there might be simpler ways of not being killed on a motor bike.

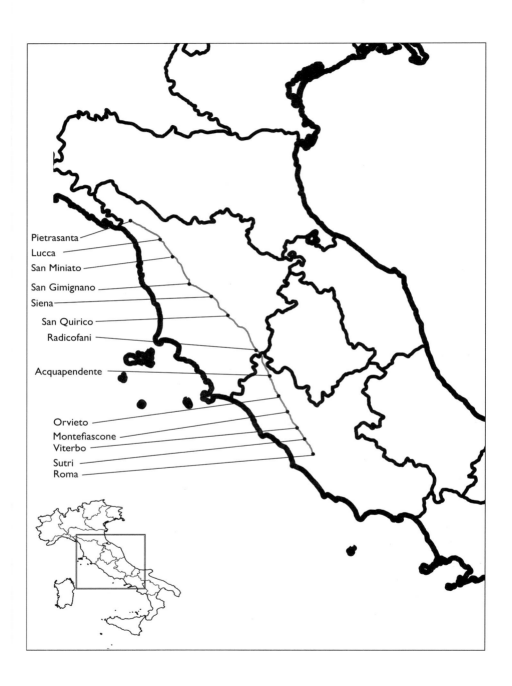

Pietrasanta
Lucca
San Miniato
San Gimignano
Siena
San Quirico
Radicofani
Acquapendente
Orvieto
Montefiascone
Viterbo
Sutri
Roma

Pietrasanta to Rome:
2nd May - 22nd June

To return to my journey.

My next task is to walk the Tuscan stretch between Pietrasanta and Lucca and then on into the marshes of the Arno Valley.

But first it is good to stay, once more, even briefly, in Pietrasanta.

My small hotel looks onto the main gate, and inside the gate is the town square which has buildings from several different centuries which blend effortlessly. On one of these is an inscription which tells us that in this house Michelangelo Buonarotti, between 27th April and Ist June 1514 drew up a new contract for the façade of San Lorenzo in Florence

For many years a single pillar, the only one that ever came to Florence of all those hewn in Pietrasanta, lay forlorn in the Piazza San Lorenzo.

It makes you think: all that time arguing and negotiating. Yes, San Lorenzo in Florence, with its unfinished brick façade, was crying out for the marble facing which Michelangelo and the local quarries could have provided. But look today and you will see that the bare ribs of San Lorenzo still wait to be enfleshed (Santa Croce and the Duomo were in the same state at that time, and it was three centuries before they were clothed). But the people of Pietrasanta were proud enough of the great genius to record his presence in their town, even for negotiations which bore no fruit.

Friday 2nd May. It is so long since I have walked that I have to make a firm decision to set off for Lucca and get back on track for Rome. The *Via Aurelia* continues down the coast to Pisa but pilgrims turned inland over Montemagno towards Lucca, which was famous amongst the Lombards, Franks and Normans. William Rufus, whose name means 'of the ruddy countenance' used to swear "Per Sanctum Vultum de Lucca" By the Holy Face (of Christ) at Lucca

Camaiore is my first and most important stop. It once had a pilgrim hospice. Sigeric stayed here in a monastery and will have seen the churches I am looking at, but each time I think of him passing by I have to imagine away such things as Romanesque campanili and doors in pilgrim churches marked IN and OUT for crowd control. These came after his time.

Montemagno is a steep, steep climb, or else I am less than fit. As I near the top of the zig-zag road, I stop and take time to read a promise, set in stone, of copious indulgences to pious pilgrims. As I do so, a local man smiles and says "You've earned them". He helps me to lean on a wall, we look at the way I've come up, and he tells me there was an ancient law ordering that the verges be cut back to the distance of a cross-bow shot, to make the way safe from robbers. It is reassuring to hear the ancient lore (and law) repeated. As we have already seen on the Cisa Pass such a decree was needed.

I've entered the Val Freddana, and the road slopes gently down to a meeting with the River Serchio. Though several hospices are named in the itineraries (Valpomano, Albiano, Plotano) I see no sign of them. The 25 kilometres to Lucca are not going to present any difficulty.

At the bridge outside the walls of Lucca, roads and river converge. A market is being held. Live animals are for sale. Attendance is entirely local and the atmosphere is lively.

I go in through the gate of San Pietro, whose name encourages Romeward-bound pilgrims. Lucca is a town to be savoured. It has enough of the medieval for any romantic, but it is encased in high walls and bastions never seen by pilgrims, once meant as a defence but now converted into a *passeggiata* which most towns would envy.

And the people use it. From its shady heights all Lucca can be seen and because of it the town has been preserved from the worst excesses of development.

Saturday 3rd May. Today I shall do the circuit of the walls, so as in some way to embrace this most enchanting of cities.

Look north, and there is the Garfagnana a mixture of lost villages which live an intensely local life, and the Bagni which from Roman times and through the days of the Grand Tour have lived off gullible hypochondriacs.

Above the gates are grass-covered balconies from which I can view the bustle of traffic coming and going like motorised ants.

Here and there the surrounds are marred by insensitive development.

As I go round, and looking inward, I can see churches with their campanili which serve as landmarks and beacons, but tallest of all seems to be the Guignini family tower which, for a crown, has a patio at 120 feet, with holm oaks for ornament and shade.

I step down a while to visit the Duomo, the church of St. Martin. I love it with its sawn-off arcaded porch which jostles for space with a neighbouring building. At one time the Porch served as shelter and gathering-place for pilgrims. These medieval churches still live and breathe with carvings which some dare to dismiss as primitive. But those with a soul to be moved declare them to have special powers. Here I am between the pages of an almanac, a story-book of carvings in both high and low relief

I pass the familiar maze, symbol of the mystery tour to Jerusalem, and I tidy my hair and compose myself to enter the church. A young man hidden behind the door informs me in "Italian for foreigners" that there is a charge, and it is payable to him.

Angrily I sail past him, condemning his knavery. I look back and see above his head, high on the inside wall, St. Martin, sculpted, on a horse, silently handing down his cloak to a beggar, and looking not at the recipient but at me. And I wish the saint would stop looking at me like that.

I creep to the cross, now enshrined in a *tempietto* (freestanding little temple) of Carrara marble and porphyry, imprisoned against theft. This beautiful wide-eyed cedarwood carving of Christ, clad in a long-sleeved tunic, far from "following you with his eyes round the room" draws you in and challenges you. Charlemagne knelt before it.

Carved, it is said, by Nicodemus, who was artistically centuries ahead of his time, it floated of its own volition from the shores of the Levant to Pisa whence oxen dragged it to its providential resting place: Lucca. Unless, that is, it was stolen by crusaders.

Close by the cathedral they have redone the treasury most sensitively, using large rooms and the nooks and crannies of an ecclesiastical building. But amongst all the delights, I have eyes only for a tiny casket made for a relic of St. Thomas a Becket, not the first nor the last Christian to be murdered for a difference with his earthly sovereign.

Here, as elsewhere on the route, Norman guilt produced a reliquary and a desire to confess a sordid tale in carving or in fresco.

I return to the wall and to the city kept safe by its saviour, whose symbol, the cross, is carried high through the streets each fourteenth of September.

Once more I can see, as no pilgrim saw, the patchwork map: the outline of tiled roofs holding the shape of the Roman amphitheatre whose inner oval has for centuries contained a market.

I go back down from the wall to visit San Frediano, a church Celtic in origin and built of stones from the amphitheatre. It has plenty from most centuries to detain the visitor, but I content myself with memories of a Saxon from Hampshire (later named Richard) who reached here on his way to Rome, caught something and died. He had impressed the locals with his virtue and his story, and was sainted and even made out to be a minor king of some sort.

There is much to detain me as I reach into the city from the wall. First the church of St. Michael (Military hero of Lombards and Normans), has a marble façade, too tall for the nave behind, so that it stands out like stage scenery liable to be knocked down by some clumsy breeze. St. Michael is perched on top while heroes and celebrities are ranged below like bric-a-brac on a mantlepiece.

I would like to seek out all there is to know about the local musicians Puccini and Boccarini, but instead, once I've been to all the churches I can visit, I'll go tomorrow to Pistoia a pilgrim city not far away, and next day continue walking south.

Sunday 4th May. Pistoia was condemned by everyone, including Dante, for its feuding. It manufactured first the *pistola* (a dagger) and then diversified into firearms.

Two things I seek to see again, the Ospedale del Ceppo, with Giovanni Della Robbia's colourful frieze of virtuous people helping the poor and lame, then I'll visit the cathedral.

Pistoia, whose patron is St. James, would welcome and help any pilgrim, but the inhabitants particularly valued the Jacobéi who were on their way to Compostella. In the cathedral is one of the richest pieces of silverwork in the whole of Italy, the altar-piece of St. James.

Someone, not I, counted the carved figures (628) and weighed it (almost a ton). Powerful man, *il Barone*.

Monday 5th May. Knowing that I am due to linger and to see friends, I shall now make a token gesture and walk on, do one more stretch to Altopascio which is deep in what were the marshlands of the Arno valley.

The raised road now runs through rich land, and the journey is too easy. I am going east, rather than south, which must be to take advantage of an established river crossing.

There are medieval tales of pilgrims lost between the marshes of Bientina and Fucecchio, who were saved by the bell in the tall Romanesque tower of Altopascio. 'La Smarita'(the lost one), they call it, though it was the pilgrims not the bell who had gone astray, and were grateful for its muffled chiming as they picked their way by ear through mist and marsh.

At Altopascio, St. James is there to greet me on the façade of the church. Inside there is a fresco of the pilgrim's friend, St. Christopher, for we are near a river crossing.

Here in Altopascio it is good to salute San Rocco again, boils and all, and I like his dog with a doughnut. Pilgrims have not forgotten the man who halted his own walk to Rome to help plague-stricken victims. He paid the price. I don't know if he reached Rome. Some legends say he didn't, nevertheless his name went far beyond

With local help I find a stretch of ancient cobbled road and touch the stones the pilgrims trod. I'm leaving one marsh and entering another, except that they have both been drained. No chance of sinking into mud.

At Gallieno they mention Castelladroni. The title puzzles me. Ponte Ladroni I could understand: thieves might lie in wait at bridges, but why a castle of thieves?

Fucecchio has a beautiful, tree-lined approach and has saved its historic centre with a ring-road. And now I lose my way. Ridiculous. I miss my turning for the bridge over the Arno, and so go twice round the town. I could have done without this, as I had planned to do no more than thirty kilometers today. Without mist or marsh I have managed to stray. I'm not the first *smarrito*, but I have no excuse.

The bridge accepts me non-judgementally, I put down my stone markers and take in the scene. The Arno flows below. San Miniato hangs on a wooded crag above, and the tower which looks down on me looks north as well as over the Val D'Elsa and the roads to Siena.

I have been totting up the distances walked since Aosta, and now I check them against the maps; not easy, since some of the roads I have taken have been by-ways.

From the Swiss border to Lucca the distance on foot by the road I have taken is roughly 320 miles and I am comfortable with the time I have taken so far; fifty-four days of which twenty-seven days of walking. Belloc, going in a line straighter than any Roman road at thirty kilometres a day, would have left me far behind, but he famously sought out one church each day for Mass, and ignored the sights. The accomplishment of a vow was the main motivation for him. His unique account is totally personal, but I have a need to explore and an amateur's weakness for art, which pilgrims could see only in churches, and now I must indulge it, and seek the company of friends. I refuse to feel guilty.

In Altopascio a motto plucked from scripture warns pilgrims, "Fides sine operibus mortua est" (faith without works is dead) and this is displayed in the market place.

The Knights of Tau had an important base here; amongst them were monks dedicated to caring for the sick and weary (*Spedalinghi*). Others of the brotherhood were builders of barges and bridges.

And now, my dues paid to pilgrimage, I returned to Florence. The omens were good: outside Santa Maria Novella, by merest chance, I met two dear friends, Robert and Maria. Had we planned to meet we might, in anticipation, have spent days co-ordinating train timetables, and anxiously waiting for one another. But this was pre-ordained and was meant to be.

Then, with another friend, I set out on a journey which was also a pilgrimage in the steps of Piero della Francesca. My companion was Fr. Michael Durand of Westminster Diocese. If you must travel with another, always choose someone who is wiser than yourself, and who likes the same things.

It has been said that the world is divided into those who believe that Piero della Francesca is the greatest of all artists (his Resurrection at Borgo San Sepolcro being the greatest picture ever painted), and those who do not understand art.

At Arezzo, in San Francesco's church, they have rescued his version of the legend of the Cross. Adam the proto-corpse is surrounded by his family who have never been to a funeral before. A nut, buried with him grows into a tree which is used and re-used till it bears the burden of Christ.

The Cross is then hidden down a well, until Helen, mother of Constantine, gets on the scent. A Jew who knows the secret is tortured and lowered down the well to retrieve it. The Cross is tried and tested and being judged authentic is handed on to Christian emperors and becomes a battle standard.

This marvellous story from the Golden Legend is not accessible to the public unless they are prepared to pay to go behind the altar. But one who attends Mass or sits quietly in the front benches may still see it perfectly well from a distance.

We continue our pilgrimage making for Borgo San Sepolcro and Monterchi. In 1905 the archetypical English traveller, Edward Hutton, said "You journey over the mountains from Arezzo for hours amid all the clear beauty of Tuscan hills that have something not Tuscan about them and at last in the valley of the Tiber you come upon a tiny city at the foot of the Appenines".

To take this route is to travel through the background of Piero's paintings. San Sepolcro, is small but, has pictures in its civic art gallery of which any city would be proud.

Piero's *Resurrection* is more than a picture which uses every new Renaissance artistic device; it relies also on mythology both pagan and Christian: the God-like figure stepping into a new world, the four sleeping soldiers falling back like a flower unfolding.

We sat for an hour before it, with no thought of moving. A woman walked by on our right, talking into her mobile phone, and passed on with sightless eyes into another room.

We went to Monterchi where, in the chapel of the walled cemetery, they once treasured the Madonna del Parto (Mary when pregnant) painted by the same master, a subject rare enough in art.

Now, after squabbles, tension and vicissitudes, it is housed in a special exhibition centre where all is explained.

Set reverently, as in a secular chapel, the picture is a staged event.

Angels, exact reverse images, draw back curtains to reveal Mary, gravid and in her ninth month, opening her dress "to prepare for the historic curtain rise of the incarnation" (Muriel Spark).

I must return to my journey, back through Arezzo to Florence whence it is only minutes by train to San Miniato Scalo, and soon I am standing on the bridge over the Arno, which is a crossroads formed by the important road through the marshes following the river route and the road from north to south which crosses by the bridge. From this point I have a choice of three routes to Siena. On a map they look like the outline of a kite. In practice the choice would be dictated by reasons of safety or hope of lodgings. But first there is a short steep climb to San Miniato which towers over the marshes and over me. This was once a strategic point, and the unlovely lords of the castle felt it necessary from time to time to sack the odd village below.

San Miniato is no longer important, but it has half a dozen churches and I share a couple of pleasant hours between them. I stop, perhaps longest in a chapel of San Rocco and San Sebastiano, restored and tastelessly frescoed in the 1960s. Mercifully they forgot to put in a damp course and, with luck, the next time I pass by, the wall decorations will have disappeared. The town is proud of its links with the Holy Roman Empire. I don't understand its history except that here popes and emperors lived out their hate-hate relationship for many centuries. There was an imperial Vicar here, and emperors even stayed here in person from time to time. The Holy Roman Empire, sometimes blessed by popes but more often excommunicated, was never genuinely Italian (if that word has any meaning) and neighbours referred to San Miniato as 'Il Tedesco' (the German). The town was considered a vaguely German enclave.

I've been slipping quietly from square to square, and in one I find some medieval shops which have sixteenth-century counters, and on a seminary wall there is a motto in *Sgraffito* (yes they had high class graffiti artists then).

Incipientibus premium promittitur perseverantibus datur.

(To those who begin the prize is promised, it's those who persevere who get it).

I qualify as a beginner, being only 350 miles into my walk, and now I have good hopes of achieving my first important goal: Rome. Before leaving San Miniato I must go up the sloping steps to the upper city and the castle because I have found some local scandal in the pages of Dante. It seems that Frederick II built the castle, and in its tallest tower he imprisoned Pier Della Vigna, his ill-starred treasurer, who had been falsely delated to him by jealous courtiers. Having climbed the tower, and now high up above the rolling countryside, leaning on a window ledge, I muse on the fate of the wretched minister, blinded and tortured, who leapt to his death and to a place in the *Inferno*. In 'Suicide Wood' his arms were turned into waving branches, where Harpies nested.

From the top of the tower, I see my way ahead (I think) and I choose out the most easterly route. Hurrying down through the town I walk down towards the River Elsa which gives its name to the whole area. I know that soon at a road-junction I shall find a tabernacle, and then I have only to reach Castel Fiorentino for a stopping point.

For years they have been restoring this shrine, with its frescoes by Benozzo Gozzoli, assistant to Fra Angelico. So I shall stop there near Castel Nuovo, as pilgrims did, and be refreshed at the shrine of the Madonna delle Tosse. St. Mary of the Cough (The cough was the first sign of the plague)

And there it is before me. But, Ahi! Disappointment: the frescoes have been bodily removed 'Per ragione di tutela' (for safe-keeping) and placed in the library of nearby Castel Fiorentino. Amazing how they can lift the decoration of entire chapels and transport them to a place of safety.

Now the chapel stands all alone, weather-proof. Pilgrim-proof, too. Benozzo Gozzoli, why do I so like this artist with a name like a brand of cheese? He is not of the first rank, and hasn't the depth of his Dominican Master, Fra Angelico. He is a highly skilled workman rather than an inspired artist. Though he is free from the bonds of the middle ages, he is too traditional to be Renaissance. He often paints to please a patron, and sometimes his religious processions look like self-conscious fashion parades. But I like him.

On the main street of the village of Castel Fiorentino is the library, and there the frescoes are safe from damp and vandals, but disengaged from pilgrims. It's not officially open, but they let me in.

I stand alone and undisturbed, and my lonely offering of a midday psalm scarcely makes up for the lack of pilgrims.

The Gothic vaulted ceiling has the four evangelists and their signs as they circle a Byzantine Christ in the apex. Where an altar might have been, there is, in a classic frame, a picture set in front of multifolded curtains, theatrically rucked by five painted angels. Piero della Francesca did it better. Central to all, Mary feeds the infant Jesus while saints on either side hold sacred conversation. On the left wall of the tiny chapel is the DORMITION, the 'Going to sleep of Mary'. She is recumbent. The apostles are in attendance. Local worthies try to hog the foreground. On the right wall an empty tomb is shown. Behind it the apostles pause non-plussed. Somehow we are drawn to look upwards to find that Mary has been effortlessly carried up, and even now sits on a heavenly throne. Benozzo never fails to please, I think.

I shall now cross country to Coiano with its Romanesque parish church, and on to Gambassi on a hill. For much of the way the nearest approximation to the *Via Francígena* takes me along farm tracks which are not straight. They go round minor hills in the most unroman way.

The places named on the map were always tiny. It is not as though they have shrunk from days of glory.

In Gambassi, by far the biggest, they do have a Pro Loco (an information and general help office) but I am their only visitor. I explain that now I am in their town centre (neat and welcoming as it is) I have lost sight of Santa Maria a Chianni which was visible before at a distance. They explain that it has hidden itself behind a corner of the hill on which the town stands, so I walk out to it and climb the steps to a church which would not be out of place in a more famous town. Tall columns, carvings and five apses; no fewer.

As I descend to take the winding route across the fields to San Gimignano, a school bus overtakes me, and from the windows, to a child, they mock my pilgrim pack. And I think of the prophet Elisha while he was leaving Jericho. Some small boys came out of the city and jeered at him saying "Go away baldy-head". When he turned round and saw them he cursed them in the name of the Lord. Then two she-bears came out of the woods and mauled forty-two of the boys. Good for you, Elisha!

The *Strada Bianca*, dusty and rutted, is used by tractors, and more than one farm-hand waves a greeting to me. I return their benisons, but just when I am sure that I have only one more hill to skirt, a gate bars my way. A notice forbids entrance. As I have no intention of back tracking, I shall, if challenged, have to act ignorant, stupid and harmless.

No need to, for presently a signpost announces a former abbey. There are even several families enjoying a visit. Here was the stopping-place for pilgrims, bishops and even Pope Eugenius when he was on his way to consecrate the Collegiata in the town ahead of us. But first I will rest at Cellole, which is just a clearing, set back from the road, a few stone houses and a miniature Romanesque gem of a church. I remember that years ago a woman here refused to open the church of Santa Maria for me though she had the key. Her successor is kindness itself, and willingly gives me a few moments in this carefully restored house of prayer. Everything is of the simplest: Celtic decoration round the little window of the apse, a slight rise to the sacred area. Even unimportant local churches echo the great churches along the road and borrow from them. But the windows are tiny, a practical precaution in this secluded place. It was rescued from ruin one hundred years years ago, its crumbling tower reduced and made into a corner baptistery. San Gimignano is in sight now, and as I take the road, I meet an old woman who shouts "Forza!" to encourage me.

The walled town is good to look at from any angle. No matter that some travellers hate it as being commercialised, packaged and overrun by tourists. Would they prefer the picturesque, disease-ridden, poverty-stricken collection of hovels described by English nineteenth-century writers?

Tourists are the life-blood, even if they clog the city. Stay long enough here, and in the off-season, or when the last day-tripper has departed, then life is pleasant enough and San Gimignano can be savoured.

So now, without prejudice, I approach the town from the north but first sit on a bench outside the wall and compose myself before undertaking the solemn ritual act of entering the city through the Porta San Matteo.

True, there were once more than seventy windowless Spartan towers staring down on the poor, and glowering at one another across the narrow streets. True, the population was nearly destroyed by the plague, and for a little while both pilgrims and merchants shunned the town. True, the people were forced to ally themselves with Siena or Florence, with Guelph or Ghibelline, and to defend themselves against neighbouring Colle di Val D'Elsa or Poggibonsi, and engage in every sordid political ruse, but through its gates entered travellers small and great, and even Dante Alighieri came here as ambassador and reconciler. He walked its narrow main street past crusader churches and pilgrim hostels and climbed the stairs to the great chamber of the Town Hall and there spoke eloquently, in a bid to reconcile warring factions. Fruitlessly as it turned out. This small but generally prosperous merchant town called in the best artists it could afford, and their work for the most part was open to be seen by visitors and pilgrims, and even its amenities, a washing place, a well, are now admired as romantic or artistic. What now is called the Piazza della Cisterna (from its central well) was once the Piazza delle Taverne, where many a thirst was quenched, and pilgrims, soldiers and merchants rested.

I'm thirsty too, and tired, I'd almost gone to sleep on the bench and so I will go in and quickly turn left down a side street to the Austin Friars who offer the simplest and most genuine of welcomes. They have long been in the Val D'Elsa. In the twelfth and thirteenth centuries there had been many hermits living in loose confederations. Francis and Dominic drew many of them in their wake, but others followed the rule of Augustine, fifth-century philosopher and roué turned bishop and saint. These the Pope caused to be formally united in a Congregation and here one of their houses nestles inside a corner of the wall.

Friendship and gratitude make me refrain from going into detail, but here religious and community life go with local pastoral work, and there is a welcome to pilgrims at the common table. In the chapter-house, now used as the chapel, the church's hours are sung. Everything is in order; even the community cat knows the sound of the final hymn, and gets up from its appointed place to lead us to the refectory. To experience modest comfort and to be part of community life is one of the perks of the clerical pilgrim. In the past too, he had the advantage over the laity who were often a prey to the thieving landlords or had to sleep in a church porch or monastery barn.

The ideal of the religious house open to every traveller was hard to maintain. Already in the ninth century monks were complaining that two or three pilgrims a day was alright "but with today's crowds St. Benedict would give orders to bar the door". And some pilgrims overstayed their welcome. "A guest and a fish: after three days, they begin to stink".

San Gimignano is half-way between Florence and Siena and was coveted by both. Pride made it call in the best artists available for its town hall and churches.

The Collegiata became the Parish Church, and to welcome pilgrims it was turned on its axis to face the *Via Francígena* which runs through the city. The new façade did not contain a central door …

It is recorded that they placed a door on the left for the men, and one on the right for women. But I think they were influenced rather by the growing custom of directing pilgrims left and right through the church when there were great numbers, to avoid tragedies such as had happened in France, when panic led to a stampede. For master-painter they hoped to have Simone Martini (think of the Maestà in the council chamber of Siena!) but he was in Avignon decorating the palace for an absentee pope. All the right-hand wall is covered with a cycle of frescoes, in the centre, a large crucifixion, and all around stories from the New Testament by Simone's "Chompagno". Who was this assistant? Was it perhaps a certain Barna da Siena, otherwise unknown, who fell from a ladder while working here, and died two days later? Or was it Memmo Lippi, Simone's brother-in-law, the local *Pictor Civicus* (Resident Artist) who had his own contract with San Gimignano, and who worked next door in the town hall? For those who could not read the Bible these paintings were a treat, nay a feast.

High up in the corner near the door is the Annuntiation: Gabriel, so gentle and respectful, almost apologising for intruding; Mary, surprised while reading her prayer-book, and so afraid; the servant outside spinning wool, pressing one ear to the partition wall and listening, eyes wide open. How else could we know what was said to Mary?

On this side there is also a chapel of Santa Fina, co-protector of the city town., a teenage anorexic who starved herself to death in 1253. The chapel is purest Florentine Renaissance. On the right her story is told. On the left her funeral and the general grief are described by none other than Ghirlandaio. For once they didn't have to search far and wide for a top artist. Domenico was a local lad.

Now I'll walk over to the left aisle which was painted by Bartolo di Fredi. The stories are from the Old Testament. The characters, the fashion and the scenery are all from the fourteenth century. Here the story of Job comes to life, and the domestic disasters over which his spirit triumphs.

I catch a glimpse also of the Last Judgement of Taddeo di Bartolo (techniques for recalling names might be useful in this church). The just he has placed in serried ranks. They are at peace (and boring); all his energy has gone into depicting the torments of the damned. He revels in scenes of hellish punishment. Gluttons, usurers and wicked women are put through their paces. Every time I enter this church I'm tempted to stay longer than last time. As I prepare to leave I see that my friend Benozzo has signed a picture. He was called in late to paint a fresco on the inside of the façade, where once the main-door had been. St. Sebastian, very full of arrows, looks slightly uncomfortable balancing on a marble pedestal while local fops and dandies strut about and pretend to shoot him. It is not one of Benozzo's best.

More artists than I could list have spent months and years on scaffolding in this church. Among resident clergy there was Baldassare Cossa who became an anti-pope, John XXIII by name, and has his tomb in Florence, in the baptistery. I'm sure he had at one time been a leader of mercenary soldiers. Life was not dull in San Gimignano. Perhaps there was need for St. Bernard, St. Francis and Savonarola to preach conversion in this very church.

I hurry back to the good friars and go into their church to sit behind the altar and see if Benozzo can redeem himself with the story of St. Augustine. The strict discipline of his early schooling, his wayward adolescence, the dogged love of his mother, the long-suffering Monica, Augustine's role as Bishop and Doctor of the Church. The Augustinian Community allows the public in not only for Mass and prayer, but also to enjoy an art-filled church.

I must now spend a day in the countryside around. I shall visit Monterriggioni and an island abbey, even though it will feature next on my walk. Previews have their purpose.

It is difficult to leave friends, and (*pace* the purists) I love San Gimignano, and so I accept the kind invitation of the friars to return when I am retracing my steps northward later in the year.

The journey continues out through the southern gate, San Giovanni. I'm going in the general direction of Poggibonsi, but, important as it once was, and though it has some remains of churches, that modern city does not attract me, and I shall turn off by Colle di Val D'Elsa, a town stacked on two levels. From habit I climb it and am rewarded by views which have become clichés. Here Franciscans and Augustinians vied with one another in showing kindness to pilgrims.

The houses of prosperous merchants still inspire admiration, but do not detain me. So on to the Abbadia a Isola, a tiny hamlet now, but once a fortified abbey on an island surrounded by a ditch and by marshes.

Yesterday I was here incognito, part of the passing trade. Today I've come here as a pilgrim, and shall ask to celebrate the evening Mass with the priest in charge. I show my "Celebret" (He may celebrate) with its coat of arms of the Cardinal of Westminster. It has opened many doors.

I will now cross the wooded hill to Monterrigioni and seek lodging for the night. It is as strange a sight now as it was to Dante and, uncluttered, it crowns the hill. When the poet sought an image for a circle of Giants cowering half submerged in Hell – he recalled Monteriggioni – its curving ramparts crowned with towers.

Sunday 1ˢᵗ June. At 8.30 a.m. I walk out through the southern gate of Monteriggioni. My pack seems heavy. Have I packed my books badly? Abbots had donkeys to carry their books. I'll walk for one hour then rest if necessary. In this, which many claim to be the most beautiful countryside in the world, it is easy to forget my load, and by 11.45 a.m. I'm on the outskirts of Siena making for the Porta Camollia. I've seen no sign that there once were forty hospices in Siena. Now there are hotels, all of them full at this season. None of my favourite stopping-places can offer me a room, so I'm obliged to pay over the odds for bland impersonal service in a large and noise-infested well-known hotel on 'La Lista'. So much for the famous motto: "Siena magis pandit portas" (Siena is most generous of all in opening its doors).

For consolation I go first to St. Dominic's Church and pay homage to the skull of St. Catherine. (From the neck downwards she is in Santa Maria Sopra Minerva next to the Pantheon in Rome.) She was not a martyr, except to the unreformed churchmen of the fourteenth century. Boldly she denounced corruption, in particular in the papal court. She journeyed to Avignon in Provence to bring back the truant pope, dragging him all unwilling back to Italy and to the See of Rome.

Time to lean on the wall next to San Domenico and take in the view of the cathedral which was constantly remodeled as ambition soared beyond means and common-sense.

Down to the family home of Catherine's merchant family, the Benincasa, now a place of pilgrimage where first I stayed in the early 1960's as a student and a guest of the good Sisters who looked after her house and shrine. It is set above the Fonte Branda where the gossips of her day flayed the washing in the large basins of one of Siena's many public fountains.

From this quarter I walk up from the gate and bow to the cathedral. I climb the steepest of city streets to stand in awe before the Palazzo Pubblico, and to envy the Sienese their civic pride. Florence may have been stronger and held a larger collection of vast and heavy palaces, but for grace Siena takes the palm. Shell-shocked by the concave beauty of the Campo, I sit and simply accept what I will never comprehend: Then I go up through a free-standing side door of that monument to overreaching vanity, the "New Extension" to the Duomo. The great and famous cathedral, with its sculptures by Maitani and Pisano, was not considered grand enough. Urged on by a spirit of rivalry with wealthy Florence, the Sienese in the fourteenth century wished to spin the whole church round and make a mere transept of the vast nave. They were foiled by three things: 1. The huge new pillars of the extension began to lean and to take the hill with them; 2. Money ran out; 3. The Plague, never quite absent from Europe, returned with devastating force in 1348 and wiped out between one third and one half of the population. Inside the cathedral as it stands today the not quite harmonious proportions nevertheless create a sense of awe though the colour scheme is designed to please lovers of liquorice allsorts.

The pulpit, both classical and popular, tells the salvation story and calls the people to repentance. But what stuns the mind and must have overwhelmed both peasant and pedant is the storied floor; a vast series of *intaglio* pictures linking pagan and Old Testament prophecy with the Christian message. I have long ago lost count of the number of times I have stayed in Siena but today I find that they have made new discoveries beneath the church. During the building of the baptistery the former entrance now beneath the dome was filled in, and therefore preserved.

Now, by melting into a group given privileged access to these discoveries I can look on frescoes last seen by medieval pilgrims as they were welcomed into the cathedral.

After a morning visit for Mass in the cathedral at a side altar, I come out and sit on the cathedral steps amongst tourists and pilgrims (which is which?) and look across to Santa Maria della Scala, which began as a refuge for foundlings and became a hospice used by all those who had survived thus far on the road to

Rome. I can remember when this was still a working hospital with ambulances outside.

Carefully restored, it is now the on-site museum of a medieval hospice. In the cellars there are records of the guilds who supported its work. Tenth-century accounts speak of a 'Zenodochium', a place for welcoming strangers (no Zenophobia here), but there is a tradition that it may have been founded two centuries earlier. Upstairs the main ward is vast and high with windows at the top to let out bad vapours. Wall- paintings describe the daily life of a busy hospital. Abandoned children are looked after by wet-nurses. Helpers, religious and lay, pass through the wards and attend to people of every age and state of health. It seems that many children did not survive infancy. Some are seen mounting a ladder (*scala*) to heaven. On this my second day I wish to visit the town hall which in the almost democractic heyday of the city may have opened its doors to pilgrims. Certainly they will have made a prayer-stop at the tabernacle in the Campo set against its massive wall, either the modest medieval shrine or the renaissance stone building we see today. In the fifteenth century they may have been drawn to join the crowd gathering to listen to Bernadine of Siena, women on one side of a modesty curtain, men on the other. Bernadine was a leading light of the Scala Hospice, fearless amid the danger of disease. Ascetic, with hollow cheeks and unique pointed jaw (see his skull in L'Aquila, where he died), he fascinated the people with sermons that pulled no punches. He castigated every vice, and the cities vied with one another to be lashed by his tongue. His banner is seen everywhere IHS, not "Jesus Hominum Salvator" (Jesus saviour of men), a common explanation, but simply the first letters of the name Jesus in Greek.

Once the visitors have gone in and up the stairs to the public rooms, St. Christopher looms over them in welcome. After a prayer in the chapel, would they care to peep round the corner and look into the map room and catch a glimpse of the Maestà of Simone Martini? I go in sit down comfortably and let it speak to me. On the opposite wall a leader of mercenaries prances across the landscape on a well- dressed horse. In the background is a fortified city. Theory is pitted against counter-theory as to authorship and date.

I go through the door beneath the painting into the council chamber, to see how the town councilors deliberated on the affairs of the commonweal, overlooked by allegories of good and bad government. On one wall justice and peace reign and we have idyllic street scenes: craftsmen crafting, ladies decorously dancing, fields yielding a gladsome harvest. On the other, violence and corruption flourish, and we see the destruction of life, limb and livelihood. Didactic realism from the brothers Lorenzetti.

I now make my way back to the inner courtyard but on the way I notice how much the Renaissance revered and almost canonised the heroes and philosophers of ancient Rome. Their images are ranged alongside the saints. I shall climb the steps of the Torre della Mangia, named after its first bell ringer, known for a glutton. There is no more elegant view in the world than that from its topmost balcony. Town and country all around remind us of what inspired the brothers Lorenzetti.

Monday 2nd June. Now I shall plunge into the countryside on which yesterday I gazed from the tower. I feel almost like running, both arms in the air, out through Porta Romana, and down the Via Cassia to Rome. The church of Santa Maria in Belem recalls Bethlehem. At Isola D'Arbia the white and green marble of the Romanesque church is masked by scaffolding, since this is a living road in constant use, at any one time parts of it will be under repair. At Cuna I follow a straight path across fields to the Grancia, a fortified Grange of the Scala Hospice in Siena which was so important and influential that it had farms and fields and granaries all around to provide food for its constant stream of guests and its resident dependents.

This farm was necessarily made safe against local thieving barons and marauding bandits. First I look into the fortified village, very solid, still agricultural, but the sort of place on which English makeover programmes will descend when they have finished ruining the rest of Tuscany.

I can see a little chapel next to the castle grange, so I knock at the door of the nearest house. With delight and charm the householder finds a key and lets me in. After due time for prayer (for we are Christians both), we look up at the frescoed cartoon of St. James: it is recorded in the *Golden Legend* that he once came back from heaven to uphold a man who had been accused of the murder of a fellow-pilgrim, and was hanging from the gibbet. San Giacomo held him long enough in suspended animation for his false accusers to repent and spare his life. I'm reminded that this *Via Romea* is equally the road to Compostella. I thank the good man, who had no thought of seeking a tip. The obol I proffer will no doubt go to the deserving poor.

Back to the *Via Cassia*. Here much that is medieval has survived in an organic way, not too cut and dried. Ponte D'Arbia has its five-arched bridge, the doorsteps of the houses have always touched the pilgrim road. These are not relics; they are signs of continuity.

I feel that the day has been long enough to fit the journey and vice-versa, and I am at Buonconvento, name of good omen. This market town claims that Duccio di Buoninsegna came out of Siena to decorate their church of St. Peter and St. Paul. They deserve the honour for they are good people (I speak as I find), but they keep their best pictures in a secure gallery. This is a market town, wall-girt to protect its store of goods and as I arrive the stalls are set out in the open space between the wall and the *Via Cassia* from which cars peel off to seek provisions and a bargain.

This time I am merely stopping to rest here, but I vow that on my return north I shall spend more time here to listen to these people.

At this point pilgrims, though ever more eager to hasten to Rome, nevertheless felt drawn by the fame of Sant'Antimo not far from Montalcino to the west. It is the romantic paragon of the remote hillside Romanesque monastery, and is still a centre of learning and devotion. I shall leave it for my return journey and go directly to San Quirico which Sigeric would call the twelfth station north of Rome. I may take the same number of walking days to get there.

This pleasant compact town has to cope with being a centre for public transport in all directions, just as it had to cope with pilgrims centuries ago. Between its gates the original streets contained everything they needed. From the proudly carved Duomo the shop-lined main street led to the hospice where pilgrims would have been glad to see the *scala* (ladder) carved on the wall near its gate indicating that it belonged to a chain of hostels. Across the road is the tiny church with just one apse and nave. Its walls are pieced by narrow slits, not windows. The walls are tapered, large ashlar stones at the base on which smaller stones are set until the curve is complete. A very ancient technique

Having found lodgings I have all day to explore another route; that going by Hospidaletto to Radicofani just the first few miles of the road through San Pellegrino in Commenda, a simple grange now given over to Agriturismo (so that visitors can stay in unspoilt countryside) and on to Hospidaletto. In the twelfth century Ugolino da Rocchione, may his name be blessed, built what was virtually a castle with church and cottages inside, such was the pilgrim's need for protection. By 1236 this also belonged to Santa Maria della Scala. I needed that little walk, and I return to rest in San Quirico. Not entirely peacefully as it happens, for, unpacking a simple evening snack I find that some *prosciutto crudo* (naturally cured ham) just bought at a local shop, is long out of date. I could have been found dead in my bed.

Friday 6th June. Rising early I go to the shop at the first opportunity and charge these scoundrels with their felony. They find it difficult to summon up any interest, and offer me another packet of meat in lieu. Scornfully I throw the rancid rashers down on the counter and turn on my heel. From the earliest days pilgrims spoke of false-hearted merchants. A malison upon them and upon all their tribe.

Today's journey is ridiculously short, but these are towns and villages I have never visited and so I shall stop in each; moreover, tonight I am to sleep in the country retreat of Pope Pius II, no less, Aeneas Silvius Piccolomini, classical scholar, diplomat and traveller. If he could make it to Scotland then the least I can do now is pay him a visit. But I make the mistake of setting out late, and by 10.00 a.m. the temperature is in the lower-thirties. A local man seeing me heavy-laden, says with sympathy, "Maestro, fa caldo!". (Sir, it is hot) and I reply "Sì, da morire". (Yes, it's a killer).

I am making for Bagno Vignoni whose warm springs were open to the merchant classes. Catherine of Siena was brought here as an ailing child to seek a cure. Fourteenth-century accounts speak of the beauty of the whole site, and the Roman classical writers spoke of it as already ancient. In the middle ages the warm, bubbling waters were divided into two basins, one for men, one for women, and roofed to keep out extremes of weather. Beside the pool stands the hotel which was one of the Piccolomini Pope's summer residences, a horse-ride from Pienza, the Renaissance town he had built to honour his own birth. Here I put down my heavy pack in a room other than the pope's. In front is the Etrusco-roman-medieval pool which has washed the feet of many a Rome-ward traveller. This small collection of houses, shops, a church and ruined mills is overlooked by two steep hills. It will be pleasant to go up this afternoon to the Castel D'Orcia. The road is not long, but it is steep. I come to the little square in front of the church, where two old ladies sit side by side on a doorstep, knitting and not knitting, eyes half-closed. Soon one of those four eyes opens wide and fixes me. Its owner springs up and leads me to the church of the Madonna del Miracolo. She takes me to a picture on a swivel; "Doppia, Doppia", she croaks through toothless gums. Yes, I understand, it is painted on both sides. Then she goes over to the Madonna and puts a two-Euro piece of her own before the statue.

"Porta Fortuna" (this brings good luck) she assures me, and waits for me to do the same. "Good luck to you, too, Signora", and I continue up to the castle. Now I can see below me in the hollow the Bagni and above them on the opposing hill the fortified village of San Biagio. It would be wrong not to visit it. So I go down into the valley and up to the other side where at the top a solid group of houses and a tiny Romanesque church crown the woods. That's enough, I've earned my rest, I come down the winding cart- track, a steep slope with hedges on either side. But I stop and break step just in time to avoid standing on the largest snake I have ever seen in the open. Green and black, long and fat with it. Out comes my camera, but in that moment a four-wheeled drive coming uphill turns the corner and spoils everything. A curse on all four-wheeled machines. At least the snake has time to escape.

Saturday 7th June. Radicofani is settled safely on the side of the hill whose flat top and watch tower dominate the valley. Here Ghino di Tacco brooded as an evil presence over the pilgrim route. More of him later.

As I approach today's goal, road-signs invite me to go west to Bagni di Philippo and to the Monastery of San Salvatore on Monte Amiata. Many pilgrims left the road for a time here because of the fame and influence of the monastery. But I shall make the shorter journey to Radicofani and stay there for two days.

The uphill road looks exposed, and one hour before midday the sun is beating down mercilessly on me, so I seek shelter beneath the gaudy canopy of a petrol station. Is it because I look covetously at a plastic chair in a shady corner that the owner invites me to come into the garage and sets me down at table and offers me a drink. Tap water tasting like champagne. By 11.30 a.m. I am struggling up the hill and at the first houses, outside the wall, I ask where I may find lodging. "Circle the town on your right, and at the furthest point you'll find they'll welcome you". He is right, and right good too is the unhurried service in the neighbouring supermarket, where the talk is all of tomorrow's First Communion celebration.

The Albergo Torre, I must mention it by name and commend it, not just for its views but for its welcome to a stranger. My hosts are also discreet, but others in the town speak of English people not unconnected with the Royal Family who come here sometimes for the horse-riding and stay in the Albergo Torre. My lips are sealed. At evening Mass Padre Elia invites me to take part in tomorrow's celebration and later shares a meal with friends in the Albergo. At sundown, I stand outside the gate of this fortified town and pilgrim-stop, and think how grateful they must have been for the safety the town offered.

Sunday 8th June. First Communion, and everything is as it should be. There is little of the ghastly charade seen elsewhere (videos and photographs, dressing up and expensive rivalry). This Pentecost celebration of the Spirit forming the church becomes a celebration of Communion and Community.

I have an invitation to a First Communion party shared by several families, but I am shy and do not know the exact time or location. While I think about this, I go up to the tower of Ghino di Tacco. He must have been an especially bloodthirsty gangster to have merited a place both in Dante's *Inferno* and Boccaccio's *Decameron*. He was a dangerous brigand of the self-deluding sort who claimed to rob the rich in order to help the poor. Pilgrims and travellers, it is true, were glad enough to pay him protection money and sleep within the safety of his den, but that does not confer on him any kind of sanctity or even humanity.

Ghino's brother in Siena had been sentenced to death by Judge Benincasa (of Catherine's family) so Ghino cut off the judge's head and fled. He then set up his tower and toll gate, mulcting everyone who passed north or south.

Pope Boniface VIII was pope at the time. The abbot of Cligni, said to be the richest man in the world, had just visited him in Rome and caught a griping of the bowels and the doctors advised him to go to the baths near Radicofani. He and his whole train (more numerous than the hangers-on of any modern celebrity) were ambushed. The abbot tried bluster and threats of excommunication, without success. And then on the table- top of the hill of Radicofani, Ghino, like a schoolboy plucking the legs off a fly, played with his prey. The remedy for the Abbot's stomach upset was dry toast and the local wine. Once cured, he was invited to a sumptuous banquet and all his train and possessions were restored to him. Suddenly, the abbot saw that this was at heart a good man. "Cursed be the fate that condemned you to so damnable an occupation!" he said to Ghino. The abbot introduced him to the pope who gave him a large Priory of the Hospitalers of which he made him a Knight, and he remained a servant of Holy Church and of the Abbot of Cligni.

As I come down from the castle, Padre Elia is getting ready to go as a guest to the common breakfast, and with him I am made welcome, and share the fish which Christians share. Amid all these good things, I am suddenly intensely homesick for friends in London, and I sense the need to be in touch, and since the hotel and everything else is closed a young couple I meet in the street offer me their mobile to get in touch. But it is the sacristan who takes me to his own parents' home where we chat and share wine and local *dolci* (sweetmeats) and I phone and get news of the death of a friend.

In the evening I walk down just below the town, where on the pilgrim road there is a post-house mentioned by Dickens. He does not speak well of it, and now it has gone to ruin since it was bought by an American speculator. Padre Elia has given me details of the unpaved road southwards across the hills, and as the sun sets I try out the first mile. I need time for thought, and I need to get my bearings. Coming back I almost stand on a snake, also bedward-bound, and he allows me to take his photograph.

Monday 9ᵗʰ June. Because of the heat I'll start walking by 8.15. Today I'm following the route of the pilgrims who stayed up top at

Radicofani and then went downhill, south towards the via Cassia. The unsurfaced road is long and there is no hiding from the sun.

Several times I have to make a choice at a fork in the road, and I look back at Ghino's tower etched against the sky-line, and try to line myself up on the bearings I took from it yesterday. I'm reassured when I meet the River Rigo and can follow it down to where it meets the *Via Cassia*.

At Novella, I have to pass the open gate of a farm which has huge barns and a pack of the nastiest mongrels I have ever seen. For half a mile they follow me. One of them leaps up and hangs by his teeth from my back-pack, his legs flapping against my shins. At last they tire of what little sport there is, and, as if they have hit some invisible boundary wall, they turn round as one and, looking back at me, they slouch off, shoulders hunched like modern urban vandals.

At the bottom of the valley on the *Via Cassia*, I sit in the shade and, in a café, treat myself to iced water. Walking on tarmac is not an improvement on the cart- tracks by which I've descended. Now the climb to Acquapendente (hanging water) rivals the angle of that to Radicofani. Here and there it includes well-marked stretches of the *Via Francígena*. A young man takes great trouble to stop his car and wait for me: "You want a lift?"

"How kind you are", I say, "but I'm walking – "E una sfida, devo sempre andare a piedi" (it's a vow I've made, I must do it all on foot). He looks at me, not a little hurt that his genuine offer has been spurned, and scarcely believing that anyone could make a vow to go anywhere on foot.

Acquapendente has its history, but has lost all its beauty. The town has been brutally raped by the motor-car, which ravages every narrow street. No effort has been made to control it. Padre Luigi, the Parish Priest, on the recommendation of Padre Elia, finds me a place at the convent of the Clarisse (Sisters of St Clare) at the highest point of the town. At Santa Chiara, I am offered the simplest of rooms, and a chance to celebrate Mass with the Sisters.

Tomorrow the road will drop down to Lake Bolsena.

Tuesday 10th June. After early Mass with the invisible Clarisse I take up the journey. Near the Porta Romana, by which the road runs south, stands Santo Sepolcro which was begun in the eleventh century and claims to be a dependency of the Anastasis Church in Jerusalem which is on the spot where Christ rose from the tomb. The nine-aisled crypt has the same ground plan, it is said, and great souvenir stones brought back by crusaders have been shaped to represent the Pretorium where Jesus was mocked by the soldiers. The medievals were great lovers of the virtual world, and here for long-distance travellers was a foretaste of Jerusalem while for those merely making for Rome here was a substitute for the distant sepulchre.

This is border country. We are leaving what Bishop Nikulaus called 'Tuscia'. Old prints of Acquapendente show a walled, gated city strung along the edge of a ravine and dominated by a castle. Hereabouts, that seems to be the formula for town-planning.

My first stopping-place is San Lorenzo Nuovo, built by Clement XIV in 1774 in time for a Holy Year. Not that there was a huge influx of pilgrims; by that time the great days were over, but carriages were constantly getting bogged down in the marshes, and people wished to sleep at night in safety from the "Mal Aria" below, which they thought was lethal.

The descent to Bolsena is through Casa Paese Vecchio (the old town) , but before reaching the shore I take a slightly higher line to the east. The indications are that the old road did not hug the marshy lakeside. My journey is longer but I gain a panoramic view. Not that any ancient pilgrim ever spoke of the view, nor does it seem to have entered into their minds to describe the scenery. True, Nikulaus of Greenland remarks on the frozen alpine lakes (was he homesick?) and Egeria the fourth-century Spanish nun was sensitive to the stark beauty of the Holy Land. She knew how to draw a word-picture of Mount Sinai. But generally pilgrims' thoughts were on their goal.

Here, however, their gossip will have been of two local attractions: first, Santa Cristina, an early Christian martyr with a lively medieval legend attached, was once Bolsena's only claim to fame, but in the thirteenth century she was o'ertopped by the Eucharistic Miracle of Bolsena which drew vast crowds and fostered devotion to the Blessed Sacrament. (More of that later).

The old town, gated and castled is built on Roman and Etruscan ruins. On the flats below and alongside the lake a not ugly new town fills the gap, and stretches as far as the first Christian settlement with its miles of underground catacombs, where fourth-century martyrs and simple Christians in their rock-carved bunk-beds take the briefest of overnight rests awaiting the imminent dawn, and the Second Coming of Christ, which is to be soon, very soon.

Cristina was only a teenager, a rebel with a cause, and chose Christ when she knew it meant torture and death. As luck, and the legend, would have it, her father was the local governor and was obliged to enforce the commands of the wicked emperor.

A decade ago I followed the crowd as the local people told the story on an evening and a morning in July. Fearlessly Cristina confronted her father, and everything the forces of evil could throw at her.

The crowd followed her statue through the streets, stopping to contemplate a series of *tableaux vivants* where enthusiastic matrons, lasses and especially local swains, posed to tell the story. Much hagiography is compensation therapy, gilding on the coffin.

We know next to nothing of Cristina, but what we see enacted is the triumph of severe determined goodness over scheming heartless evil, represented in one scene by live serpents. On her father's orders, Cristina, chained by the feet to a boulder, is thrown into Lake Bolsena, but the rock floats and like Venus she is carried to the shore. Proof of this is to be seen to this day at her shrine where the very stone, marked with her footprints underpins the altar.

Today, as I stand before the canopied altar, I think of the Bohemian priest who in 1263 made a long journey to Rome wracked by doubts about the presence of Christ in the eucharist. Recently, there had been a huge increase in devotion and he found no way of warming to it. I should add that by the thirteenth century practically no lay people received the consecrated bread and wine at Mass. They were unworthy and had to be commanded to receive communion (preceded by confession) once a year at Easter.

None obeyed Christ's command to drink from the chalice. But from afar they worshipped intensely. Once, when the priest, facing the altar, raised the sacred host but slightly, they cried "Altius Johanne!" ("Higher, Father John!"). Now on his way back from Rome, still uncomforted, the Bohemian came near to the summer retreat of the popes at Orvieto. Here, by the lake, he celebrated Mass at the altar of Santa Cristina. As he blessed and broke the bread, he saw blood flow and stain the linen and the altar. Pope Urban IV was told and ordered that these be treasured, and that a great cathedral be constructed and adorned in Orvieto to receive the linen and the pilgrims.

But I see a difficulty here. Such devotion is clean contrary to the Gospel and to Christ's intention. Those who were persuaded to believe in Christ's presence because the consecrated bread, when broken open, released blood, are like Thomas who says, "I'll believe if I can have visible tangible proof".

Transubstantiation may not be the catchword on everyone's lips, nor is the theory easily understood, but at least it is an honest attempt to put a deep mystery in human words. Christ gives himself in the form of bread and wine which will always taste and look like bread and wine. He does not promise Haemoglobin.

There are worse examples of gruesome realism in Italy. Lanciano in Abruzzo has human cartilage preserved in a crystal monstrance. Blessed are those who have not seen.

But here in Bolsena this prayerful church with its nine interconnected areas of prayer strengthens faith with its early carvings and its sense of continuous welcome to pilgrims. St. Roch was here, and, it is said, received temporary relief from his pains.

In a quiet moment in the chapel of Santa Cristina which is at the entrance to the catacombs, I find it humbling to claim a blood relationship through the Eucharist with the anonymous Christians who knew that to profess Christ was to risk death. I think also of victims of religious and ethnic pogroms down the ages, and the length of time it takes before anyone feels guilty about them.

Whilst here I can even understand, I think, how the Bohemian priest envied those who seemed to believe so easily and was convinced by signs which Christ never promised. But I can also sympathise with the great St. Thomas, Dominican and razor-sharp theologian, who laboured to fine-tune a theory which gave insight into a great mystery, only to be upstaged by a gross popular travesty of what Christ had taught. At the pope's behest he composed the official hymn for the feast of Corpus Domini, but he used it to hammer home the Church's true teaching.

> Visus tactus gustus in te fallitur
> (Sight touch and taste cannot cope)

> Sed auditu solo tuto creditur
> (We rely entirely on Christ's word)

Peace. I've had my say. This is a holy place. I'm fortunate to be here.

Before I leave Bolsena, I must pay homage to Pope Martin IV, and so I go to the restaurant which stands on piles over the waters of the lake and order from the menu what he ordered on that fateful night of 28th March 1285, *Anguille alla Vernaccia,* eels marinaded in white wine. He died next day.

Wednesday 11th June. It is only 9 miles to Montefiascone, which dominates the southern end of the lake. The old road generally kept higher than this new road, but not entirely. Well informed sign-posts make the right historical connections. "Ponte Romano", says a sign.

Now bridges are the most permanent of relics. They are organic. They have a life of their own. This bridge has been honourably retired and is smothered in greenery. On all this stretch there are Roman ruins, which did not escape the notice of pilgrims who used their imagination and Christianised them.

Before I know it, I'm standing on sacred ground, San Flaviano on the *Via Cassia*, a church full of character. It is on two levels with light pouring into its heart, full of carvings which appear weird to us, where demons fight, and ugly is the new beautiful. I like the challenge of Lombard and Romanesque art. It does not speak to our intellect, but hits us in the solar plexus where, as Origen tells us, the emotions reside. To point out the obvious connections with local Etruscan art is only to say that emotions can be deeper than thought.

There are frescoes too, some in narrative style. Two knights richly bedight and all insouciant, go a-hunting in the forest, only to meet two skeletons. A hermit warns them, "Think of what you are and of what you cannot avoid becoming".

And then there is the famous tombstone, which I recollect, over forty years ago, used to be in the body of the church near a pillar, but is now behind an iron gate in a side chapel. The stone is friable, the inscription illegible. No matter, I have it by heart:

EST EST EST. PROPTER NIMUM EST
JOHANNES DE FUCRO DOMINUS MEUS
MORTUUS EST
(Est Est Est On account of a surfeit of Est, Johann de Fugger, my master, has died)

In 1114, Bishop Johann de Fugger was on his way from the north to pay his respects to the pope. At every stage he sent his servant Martin ahead to sample the local wine at the inns in the towns where he would stay.

"EST" chalked on the wall of a hostelry meant: "It is drinkable" and the Bishop might stay the night. But when Martin got to

Montefiascone (the Hill of the flask) "EST EST EST" was the comment of this early-day Michelin Guide.

The Bishop stayed and drank. And drank. And stayed to drink himself to death, stating in his will that every year a barrel of the local wine should be poured over his grave.

I've seen the story acted out here in a (recently-created) medieval pageant. They play down the bishop element and call him "Il Barone de Fuk". Good business sense dictates that at the same time there be a wine-tasting on a well-marked route from Cantina to Cantina to the number of ten. This I once followed religiously with a sapient friend, and nothing could have been more orderly.

The remark of the Etruscanologist Dennis here holds good: "The story is better than the wine", for the supply of local wine has to expand to sate the thirst of those who wish to savour the story.

Now I enter through a Baroque gate, and a steep main street leads to the Borgo and the Duomo of which the citizens are inordinately proud. Its dome is the third biggest in Italy and looks good from a distance. Walking round the cavernous interior I stop in a side chapel and exchange looks with two recumbent Baroque bishops.

In comfortable enbonpoint they recline on one elbow like Etruscans at their last banquet. One of them, Valerio Tartanno Falisco (1545) was, we are told 'Stoicae Pietatis" (of stoic piety). It doesn't show.

As I leave I see a flier for a pilgrimage to S. Gabriele Adolorato in the far away Abruzzi mountains. The need to be elsewhere! My present aim is much more modest. Rome is only walking distance away.

Thursday 12th June. Going down and passing once more by San Flaviano I enter for a short prayer. A prancing St. George flickers across the altar of the lower church.

On the *Via Cassia* Viterbo is immediately visible. It will not have been the goal of early pilgrims. They made slightly to the west, to the sulphur baths of Bullicame which were open to the public. In Dante's time they were also the haunt of prostitutes. Nowadays they are once more respectable and I find them easily enough, which is more than Abbot Nikulaus did. Indeed, what with local accents and well-meant directions he confused them with baths near Orvieto a few miles back. Sigeric, as he came north, had difficulty too, though he did find the same bridges I am crossing today.

I do not understand the attraction of chemicals bubbling up from these sandy flatlands, but they say that if a thing is nasty and stinks it is good for you. Signposts pointing to the exclusive papal baths nearby endorse the theory, almost canonise it.

The Baths may be flourishing but the Romanesque church of Santa Maria di Forcassi is ruined; only the triple apse remains to remind us that once this was the route. Gradually Viterbo began to draw the people away from the plain. I have time to re-trace my steps and do as later pilgrims did, seeking the safety and reflected glory of the papal presence in Viterbo, that is, if the pope was not away crusading or meeting emperors or even, occasionally, visiting Rome to do his daytime job.

The road lifts me towards the curtain walls (3 miles of them) and the gate beneath the palace. Had I been toiling up the hill in 1460 I might have seen Aeneas Silvius Piccolomini (Pope Pius II) taking a ride out into the countryside, benignly acknowledging travellers and peasants and enquiring about the crops.

This city boasts a long list of resident popes. The list of their virtues is shorter. Here they hoped to escape the heat, dirt and disease of Rome and the bitter rivalry of the Frangipani and Orsini families. The English Pope, Nicholas Breakspeare, took refuge here from the Emperor Frederick Barbarossa.

Simple travellers were glad of a choice of four hospices, whilst the Knights Templar gave a sense of security to the city. I ask for a room in the *Golden Lion*, simplest of hotels where they have made me welcome more than once before.

Friday 13th June. Viterbo is proud of its roots. I'll stay a day and wander. First the medieval quarter, with many a stone staircase and balcony. It would look genuine if it were not crawling with film crews looking for the authentic. I wonder at the name San Pellegrino: perhaps some pilgrim died on his way to Rome and received the consolation prize of sainthood, to which a legend soon attached itself while miracles followed.

But this town can offer much better: Santa Rosa, a young woman who in 1233, having heard the message of St. Francis stood up in public and preached not only the value of poverty, but justice for the poor. This was dangerous. The Emperor Frederick II expelled her, as a menace to the common good, to remote Soriano nel Cimino. She tried to join the Poor Clares, but in her life-time they never admitted her to their Franciscan order. Later, her miracles, her tragically short life, and her posthumous fame caused them to re-write history and to claim her as their own, and now her macabre remains are exposed in a vast soulless classical church.

In the same way, many a good person has lacked support from church or state, until after death, when the people have vied with one another to honour the sainted corpse.

Now I must go and seek out the famous "Macchine", those towering creations in papier maché, topped by a statue, renewed or replaced over the centuries, some of them ninety feet high, which are hauled on the shoulders of Fachini (porters) through the streets of Viterbo to the joyous welcome of the crowds each year in early September.

The Rome-ward pilgrimage has its own value but any pilgrim likes something extra, something local, something different. Viterbo is happy to offer it.

From the eastern side of the city I walk towards the Papal Palace wishing to track down a bit of English-Norman history which I have missed on other visits because I did not think a little Jesuit church could hold the clue - but the Gesù was once San Silvestro and that church witnessed a foul murder.

Henry Earl of Cornwall, first cousin of the future Edward I, was returning from a war with the Turks in North Africa; royalty returning from similar skirmishes requisitioned the surrounding churches in central Viterbo. Ten years before, his brother Edward had overcome Simon de Montfort, once a contender for the throne, and had him beheaded. Seeking revenge, Simon's sons, Guy and Simon, burst into San Silvestro. The innocent Henry who had not even been at the battle of Evesham clung desperately to the altar and was hacked to pieces.

Dante, who had probably bathed at Bullicame, in his *Inferno* caused Guy de Montfort to be plunged into the lake to boil for ever. I move on and find that the Papal Palace, not for the first time in history, is closed for restoration. Here it is said in the conclave of 1271 the cardinals took time in their deliberations. To persuade them to hurry up the people removed the roof and the electors has to live in tents. I peep through a window and search for the holes made in the floor for tent-pegs, and then I remember that though in the nineteenth century these were pointed out to visitors as proof that the cardinals had the roof removed from over their heads, the floor was replaced and such proof as they afforded was allowed to disappear

And so must I. Tomorrow Vetralla and Capranica.

Saturday 14th June. Having been drawn to the papal city, I'll now return to the Roman road and to the path used by the earliest pilgrims. On the steep sanctuary steps of the church of San Sisto, I sit and say morning prayer. The church was bombed in 1944. Only the solid presbytery and crypt remained, and the rounded apse which is bonded with the city wall.

Down from the city the road curves like a race-track, and I am the only biped foolish enough to be on it. I can look down across the fields and see the path trod by Sigeric as he went north. He didn't have to dodge speeding vehicles, as he made for a dip in the sulphur of Bullicame.

Once on the *Via Cassia*, I know that I am on the less interesting way south because later pilgrims, once they had gone up to Viterbo kept to the heights and went by the volcanic Lago di Vico. I'll do that some other time. Here on the flat road Vetralla makes no excuse for its quiet existence. It is quite comfortable, thank you.

On the outskirts the church of San Francesco is open for business, as this is the season of Corpus Christi (the feast of the Blessed Sacrament) and I think devotion ought to be strong here if anywhere. They have exposition of the Blessed Sacrament, a bonus which a few locals are happy to take. So, midday prayer and then a visit to the early pieced-together crypt. Back in the church, people quietly come and go, and after a while I slip out onto the road which leads south through the town. There are some imposing sixteenth- and seventeenth-century palaces here and the place probably grew up around them.

I think of the pilgrims who knew they were at last only a few days away from Rome, and, not for the first time, I feel that I really do not qualify to be among them. It is they who are real. I am the ghost.

Whatever their imperfections, they were totally immersed in pilgrimage. However often they went astray, Rome was their goal. I, however, have several modern lifelines. I can magically summon help by phone. I can talk directly with my family and friends in England from time to time. Though I am walking every yard of the way (some of the medievals had horses, or at least donkeys) I have sometimes hitched back to a safe and comfortable base at night and next day come back by public transport to restart where I left off the day before.

I see no lodging here. So I phone the good people at the *White Lion* in Viterbo; no trouble, I can stay a further night there.

Sunday 15th June. Early Mass in the cathedral, in the name of the Trinity. Then there is a bus I can take down the *Via Cassia*. The five stones I have left in the shape of a cross lie undisturbed, though a woman waiting for a bus wonders why I am picking them up and putting them in my pocket.

On the road between Vetralla and Capranica there is a signpost pointing with total certainty to the Oak of Orlando. This is *Chanson de Geste* country and the troubadours sang about it.

Capranica, no more than Vetralla, does not depend on pilgrims or tourists. Immensely rich local grandees built lavish country houses and peasants clustered round. Travellers were attended to and sent on their way. Capranica has more churches than they or I can cope with. At least one is an art gallery. On the main square they have re-used the portal of an old church as an entrance to the civic hospital.

Tonight's goal is Sutri, which to my shame I had not heard of. But I've recently learnt enough about it to make it a serious stopping place.

The approach to the walled town is flanked by the ruins of its very ancient beginnings. I do not know how these have survived so near to a highway. You can touch the walls of cave-tombs and a cave-church. There are ivy-clad ruins and an Etruscan Amphitheatre. If I sit down for a long time it is not because I am tired; (I have walked only 4 miles) but because it is hard to take it all in.

I go into Sutri by the Porta Franceta whose name is a variant of *Francígena*. Through narrow streets I pass tiny sandstone churches and a Carmelite convent and come to the central square with its cafes and arches, whence I'm directed to the Hotel Sutrium. "Of course you may stay, and here is the key to the front door, which simple room would I like?"

Monday 16ᵗʰ June. While I'm handing out medals to hospitable people, perhaps I should mention not only the Carmelites but also the local curate and above all the library staff at Sutri. They know their history. We touch on every legend, and by the end of my listening I am more confused than ever. Every library should be a place of handing on local myths. I listen spellbound but detached

111

as Camillus vents his fury, as Charlemagne is awarded yet another castle and more oak trees are assigned to Orlando than ever were to Charles II of England. This is history free from the chains of chronology. All legend is advertising and the *Via Francígena* needs its billboards in any age.

Briefly, Sutrium was relatively important at certain times. The Etruscans grew too comfortable there, furious Camillus sacked it, Christians adopted it and Byzantines and Lombards coveted it.

Pilgrims called it the antechamber of Rome. There are reminders, both pagan and Christian, of all these things. For example, Furius Camillus who imposed Roman rule by force, is given a monument and Anthony the Hermit has a statue of his own near the northern gate.

The Duomo looks modern (that is, Baroque) and it is not too gross of its type. Clearly In the nineteenth Century they once deliberated whether to strip it down to its Romanesque bare bones, but here perhaps sanity prevailed.

On one pillar the plaster has been discreetly removed, enough to show the tuffa column it encases. That is all. It is for the best.

For meditation and for pilgrim links I go down to the crypt, but find it spoilt by concrete pylons. I suppose they are supporting the massive tower they added to the old church. Ah me!

They have a crucifix which was stolen and returned, which adds to its value.

In the evening, though the sky is clear blue, there is a rolling of thunder, and clouds gather as I enter the little church of San Silvestro. As Mass begins, hail rattles on the tiles which protect us. The lights go out, rain drums on the roof. Silence and total darkness in the church. Then the blue neon halo over the crucifix flickers and comes to life. The danger is past, and there is a deep communal sigh, "Miracolo".

I should have known. We are in the chapel of San Silvestro, the wonder-worker of Monte Soracte or Soratte, a hill 20 miles to the east which has influence over all the countryside. On a clear winter's day, it was admired from Rome by Horace. "Vides ut alta stet nive candidum Soracte" (see how lofty Soratte stands whitened with snow). Many regions in Italy are dominated by one mountain, which, over the centuries, is remembered in local lore.

In the middle ages San Silvestro was its guardian genius. In the fourth century he had presided over the magical transference of power from pagan Rome to the Christian church. He became pope in the time of Constantine and blessed the fateful marriage of Papacy to Empire. And so tonight a saint who could do this could surely wave his protective wand over mere local peasants and me, worshipping in his own little temple.

Now I entrust to him the rest of my journey with special reference to thunder, hail and lightning.

Tuesday 17th June. I wish to enter Rome on Sunday. I have time to explore Sutri and Veio. Today's walk begins with the antique town below. Ploughed fields contain ruins from most centuries.

Santa Maria in Parto (Mary in Childbirth), of this church, nothing is visible from the road, only crude square-cut windows in the cliff-face. Pagan followers of the Mithraic cult had first hollowed out a cave from the living rock. Long stone benches line the walls, leaving only a narrow nave which led formerly to the sacrificial stone, but now to a Christian altar.

It is light-years and a whole theology away from the Christian basilica, but it is deeply Christian.

From the womb and from the tomb we enter into life. In the vestibule, necessary to accommodate the many pilgrims, there is a fresco of Mary and the bambino, wrapped for all the world like a chrysalis.

There are also simple but lively scenes of pilgrims on the holy mountain of St. Michael in the far away Gargano peninsula, launch-pad for the Holy Land. They wear the most fetching large sun-hats. One, at least, does part of the pilgrimage on his knees.

In the picture I can make out arrows which are directed at some monster, god or demon, who tastes the wrath of St. Michael.

These, in picture form, are stories Jacobei pilgrims traded as they met those coming from the north, and I'm grateful for this sharing with them which bridges centuries, and I promise to remember them as I pass through Rome, and make for the Adriatic coast.

For today Settevenne will do. Very soon I stop at a tiny lake, which some despise and George Dennis called dreary. Here Nicholas Brakespeare, the English Pope, out-stared the Emperor Frederick Redbeard but gained no good of it, and on this road when it was less frequented Pope Innocent X, while out on his horse, was murdered by thugs. Or at least that's what local people told me.

Settevenne was once a staging post and turnpike, which are now replaced by an ugly fast-food café and a rudimentary hotel. Here I shall halt and turn aside to visit Lake Bracciano for reasons which predate Christian pilgrimage, for this was a sacred lake, volcanic and moody when the Roman Republic was still young and unsure which gods to worship. The pilgrim route from the Atlantic shore of Spain was already well-established and proof of this are souvenir mugs unearthed on the lake-shore which once had been sold to pagan pilgrims. They are now kept in the Museo Massimo near Diocletian's Baths and the Termini station in Rome. These mugs were both a reminder of the road travelled and a guideline for the way back since the pilgrim-stops, many of the names readily recognizable even today, were inscribed on the side.

Today such a mug would have neither attraction nor purpose, since pilgrims are now lifted up from their native patch and landed by helicopter, as it were, in St. Peter's Square and they do not know that they have left their own back-yard.

The *Via Cassia* once ranked among the proudest of Roman roads not far behind the *Appia,* the *Flaminia,* and the *Aurelia* in importance. Now, it is a sad disgrace. It does not lack traffic, but channels it by means of a wall of huge, ugly, concrete slabs nearly five feet high right down the middle for mile upon mile.

114

This prevents murderous drivers from mutual slaughter, which is all that can be said in its favour. By early afternoon I have other concerns. Lightning plays over the hills to the east towards Soratte. I do not like it. There is no shelter, and the cloud above is black and heavy and I am the tallest object in the landscape (I speak not to boast).

I remember my vow to San Silvestro, quicken my step and lengthen my stride.

At a petrol-station a mile ahead, the attendant says, "No, the storm will stay in the hills", and I walk on, apologising to the holy pope for my lack of faith.

I know I shall make only one more stop before Rome, La Storta, where St. Ignatius, the founder of the Jesuits, rested in 1537 when he sought approval for his Order from the pope. A little chapel marks the spot where he prayed and was rewarded with a vision of God the Father (no less) who told him, "I will be favourable to you in Rome".

The chapel is open, and people are praying before the monstrance. Home from home. Across the road from it I know I can find lodgings. They are never over-crowded, they say. It is too far from Rome to serve as a base to see that city, and people are not interested enough in local ruins to stay here overnight.

But I am, and I stay. I must look out Veio Romano which claims that in history's lottery it might have rivaled Rome. Which is why it is now a Romantic ruin.

A poster says there are guided tours of the ruins of Veio, so I walk down toward it by country lanes which feel as remote as furthest Devon, yet are only a short day's walk from Rome – typical Etruscan cliffs, caves and crumbling ruins, temples hidden in woods, everything in suspended decadence.

Then, oh dear! Enthusiasts arrive by car; a guide with a key greets us. Assembled students and amateurs declare their intention to re-enact the story of the place for us. The gods preserve us, why could we not have been left to wander and to use our imagination?

115

"Here we have a paleolithic site", we are told, and while we stand in the shade of a tree there, young people bash things with bits of stone and make noises with sticks to simulate music, and generally act paleolithically. They accompany the party over fields and through woods, and on a given cue would try to persuade us that they are Etruscans a-dancing. By keeping as far away as is polite, I manage to take in something of the site where Veio died, because in the nest that was Etruria the cuckoo that was Rome had laid her egg.

Sunday 22nd June. La Storta, the twisted one, is merely a kink in a long straight road. I am well placed to arrive for the noon-time Angelus in St. Peter's Square, Rome

The road ahead is the *Via Triomphale*.

For pilgrims the excitement was growing.

They called the last stage (as it crossed Monte Mario) the Monte Gioioso and no wonder. I sense something of their elation, after forty-six days on the road, and one hundred off it; a fair allocation if a pilgrim is to find time both for prayer and dissipation. It is not by chance that large hospitals line the road. They have always been there, and, as I expected, I find a Lazaretto (Leprosy hostel), about a mile distant from the approach to the city. Almost everywhere lepers were held at the equivalent of an arm's length from the inhabited quarter.

It was about here that pilgrims, for so long mutually supportive companions, now became rivals in the race to be first to see St. Peter's. I remember in the 1960s, journeying through France with my brother Peter, and France, his wife of Gallic origin. To while away the hours we played 'prime du clocher', the one who first saw the bell-tower of each village church gained great kudos.

So it was that in the surnameless middle-ages a pilgrim who of his group first saw St. Peter's campanile (not the dome, that came after the great days of pilgrimage) proudly took for himself and his descendants the nickname King, Konig or Leroi, the origin of many a family name. How else could peasant or merchant arrive upon a name signifying royalty, and what blood-royal family would use such a nickname?

Others, who at least arrived safely in Rome handed on the name Peregrine, Pellegrino, Pelerin, or more specifically Romeo.

On this journey my first view of St. Peter's is through greenery, though I know I could see it free-standing if I backtracked to a higher point on the left. No matter, I have a rendez-vous with His Holiness John Paul II.

Now on the flat I can see the Leonine wall which surrounds the Vatican and I stop in a large modern church to get the last blessing of a Sunday Mass. Round an angle of the sloping brick wall I come upon the wide path which will lead to Bernini's colonade.

Tables laden with tawdry nick-nacks bar the way to traffic; and invite the pilgrim to barter for a three-dimensional Botticelli's Venus, a luminous David by Michelangelo, a Da Vinci Last Supper moulded in high plastic relief. Where else can I be but Rome?

I hurry on past St. Anne's gate, and at last stand under the colonnade. A tannoy announcement is made: "His Holiness will not be giving his blessing today. He has flown to Bosnia". So! I walk all the way from Switzerland to see him and he goes off to Bosnia.

But then I tell myself that this Angelus at midday every Sunday is not an old custom in papal terms. The popes have had their permanent residence here for only 130 years, and even then they went off to the hills during the summer.

Before that they were on the Quirinal in central Rome. Officially, for many centuries, they had lived next to St. John Lateran, their cathedral.

Several popes never saw Rome, some avoided it by choice, some lived in enforced exile. Two dozen at least preferred the hill-top towns of Latium north and south of Rome, for seventy years popes lived in France. So how many pilgrims, I ask myself, especially in the middle ages, had a pope to greet them as they arrived at St. Peter's? Probably none.

So I say to myself my way of consolation, "Now, I'll make a visit *ad Limina Apostolorum* (to the threshold of the Apostles) in this case the tomb of Peter", and I walk past a fountain towards the Basilica. But then I realise I cannot. Not with those electronic machines they have, and me carrying a back pack.

It is almost as though pilgrims are unwelcome.

For a while I sit under the colonnade, and then make for the Borgo in Sassia, the quarter recently desecrated by Mussolini as he destroyed medieval streets and the studios of Bramante and Michelangelo, to make way for the *Via della Conciliazione*, jewel of Fascist town planning.

Not a stone would be recognised by Alfred. Though this was the Saxon burgh colonized by Anglo-Saxon pilgrims from the eighth century, stretching from the Hospital of Santo Spirito on Tiber bank right up to old St. Peter's. Way below our feet their dreams and their history are buried. Benedict Biscop from Northumbria in 653 was the first recorded, and he returned six times, and saw the Pantheon still covered in golden tiles. Wilfrid stayed here to make sure that Peter, heaven's doorkeeper knew him. Many a Saxon King and Queen made the journey. Caedivalla of Wessex abdicated, came here, took the name of Peter and was content to die so near the gate of heaven.

But nothing remains to witness to a thriving, if transient community. Indeed by the time of the first Jubilee the area had been several times razed and reduced to ashes.

In the fourteenth century what would become of English pilgrims as they arrived for the new Jubilees? Would they be at the mercy of Innkeepers and Charlatans? To tackle this problem John and Alice Shepherd, Rosary-sellers, transformed their little house into a hostel for English pilgrims, and I shall, at a few stages removed, enjoy their hospitality at the Venerable English College.

Roman Sojourn: 22nd June-9th July

I'll tackle the mystery of Rome by taking one-day walks, weaving in and out of its pilgrim history. "Did you do the seven churches?", they ask returning pilgrims. It is still done, though package pilgrimages tend to offer only the big four: St. Peter's, St. Paul's, St. Mary Major and St. John Lateran, each with its Holy Door, which is opened only for Jubilees. But there are also St. Lawrence, Santa Croce and St. Sebastian. The custom of doing this twelve-mile walk with prayers, confession and communion for the purpose of gaining indulgences is traced by some back to the seventh century. They mention that St. Begga, mother of Pipin, did all seven. She died in 698. St. Brigid of Sweden did it in the fourteenth century. But it was that indefatigable walker, St. Philip Neri (who was a blessing to all he met), who popularized this walk in the sixteenth century.

It is said that he did seven churches every night for ten years, accompanied by his spiritual sons and bands of youth, sometimes as many as 2,000 together. I have prayers and breakfast behind me, and all day ahead of me as I leave the company of the English College and follow the *Via dei Pelegrini* to the Tiber and to St. Peter's. Most people did the churches clockwise, but I shall defy the omens and do it widdershins. It was on this street, if anywhere, that medieval pilgrims might have glimpsed the pope in his carriage or in procession between the Lateran (his home and workplace) and St. Peter's.

I cross the river and go immediately to St. Peter's. I tell myself not to linger. There are rules, and there are seven churches to be visited. I do not find the temple of St. Peter's remotely beautiful. Not only are its proportions seriously skewed, its message is not particularly Christian. I would have felt so much more at home in old St. Peter's.

There used to be thirty-five steps up to old St. Peter's, eight years' indulgence for each. I know that because I'm sitting in the shade, on the base of a column, reading my fifteenth-century pilgrim's guide to the principal churches of Rome, written by Brewyn, chantry priest in Canterbury. He knew his Rome, having lived there under two popes. His book, compiled at a time when the Reformation was in full swing, makes no concessions to doubters, and records medieval legends with total credulity, accepting medieval forgeries with unwavering faith.

It is not unique. Many such guides existed, and it has a lot in common with the *Mirabilia urbis Romae* which Sigeric may have used in the tenth century, as he set out from the Saxon Quarter of Rome and hastened round twenty-three churches in two days, in addition to having lunch at the Lateran and collecting his *pallium* from Pope John XV. This then will be my Rough Guide, with its system of star ratings, because it assigns to each church its exact spiritual value, expressed in terms of indulgences. There is a well-established pecking-order, a divine economy. The four leading churches guaranteed 1000 year's indulgence (seasonal and connected to the great feasts), plus forty-eight quarantines (a penance of forty days related to the Lenten fast). Pilgrims who seized the main chance might have up to one third remission of sins.

I must tackle this whole question of purgatory and indulgences sometime, but now I cross the square quickly and I nip into St.Peter's just ahead of one group who are flowing uphill from a coach, and join the one-way system through a narrow gorge of metal detectors. Everything is on a scale intended to overawe the visitor. As I try to walk round another group who are comparing the lengths of rival temples marked in the marble floor I go too near a pillar, and find myself apologizing to a naked six foot-tall baby who is busy holding up a water-stoop. These pagan cherubs have invaded every Catholic church like a plague of modern teddy-bears. The disease can be traced to the artists who fell in love with the fat *putti* and grotesques which were unearthed when Nero's "Domus Aurea" (Golden House) was discovered and plundered in Renaissance times.

Now every church in Italy which has any pretensions at all must be adorned with them. They run, float and squat round the rims and ledges, wearing ludicrous pigeon's wings and nothing else.

Medieval pilgrims were spared the sight of them. I go on and lean over the marble balustrade of the Confession (the sacred central area where pilgrims pray) and I greet the pauper Simon Peter who is, I am sure, buried deep down below. Of that there can be no doubt, why else was there competition to be buried close to him, and why should this most awkward site on a hillside be chosen for the very precise placing of a memorial and for a Basilica? Could the expatriate fisherman have imagined such glory for himself as he struggled to lead the tiny community which belonged and did not belong to the Jewish settlement by the Tiber port? What were his thoughts as he died, a scapegoat for Nero's fire? "O Lord save my life, for in death there is no remembrance of you". I share a psalm he knew. (Ps. 6.)

I shall read one Penitential Psalm at each of the churches, preferring to emote with Peter rather than recite prescribed prayers to gain the papal indulgence. I am beginning to warm once more to Peter and for his sake perhaps I can tolerate the gross exaggeration of the glorious dome and the baldacchino built to the glory of man.

I go and visit Pope John XXIII, now in a glass coffin, most lovable of Popes (though the competition is not great). In my time as a student in Rome he was known for his surprise visits, partly on foot, to every quarter of Rome. Today this moment is like having

121

a quiet word with a friend before setting off to do a day's work. Then I go straight down the vast nave out into the bright morning sunlight and I slip through Bernini's colonnade and go down to the Tiber. No stopping, no sightseeing, except to look up at the Regina Coeli prison, where good Pope John made his first pastoral visit as Bishop of Rome. Here he managed to find something in common with the inmates, recalling that one of his relatives had been before the magistrates for a gun-licence offence. It is easy to follow the river seawards, where pilgrims will have walked by on the muddy banks of the yellow Tiber. I follow the ugly embankment then leave the city by the Porta Ostiense as Paul did, and seek his church which may in its restored state resemble the church of Constantine. Arch, apse and mosaics survived the disastrous folly of a workman who in 1823 left charcoal smouldering on the roof beneath a cauldron of tar. That night Pius VII lay dying, he who had been a monk of this community of St. Paul's. They did not tell him. The news would have killed him. He died anyway.

The triumphal arch with its ferocious judgemental Christ survived the fire. The medieval candlestick on the sanctuary steps is covered with contorted monsters worn smooth by the fingers of many a pilgrim. To the Confession, then, where I make my own the psalmist's prayer and ask the Lord to direct me which way I should go (Ps. 32). First I have to weave my way through the crowd who have backed up behind me, and who are looking up at the roundels with portraits of the Popes which line the architrave. "When all the spaces are filled", says the guide, "the world will end". What tosh! Who said so? Anyway, there's room for an indefinite number of heads, and in the last two centuries three Popes have clocked up eighty-three years between them.

A curious medieval tradition existed that if you went every Sunday for a year to St Paul's you got the same indulgence as those who went to St James of Spain (Compostella). We are talking mega indulgences, since this was the acme of all pilgrimages, than which non greater.

Once outside, I pick up the *Via delle Sette Chiese*, the route the pilgrims took, and I must get to St. Sebastian and it's catacombs before they close the door at twelve noon. Why this cemetery and not others? Certainly it was always important, and it claims it held the heads of Peter and Paul for safe keeping during Saracen raids.

It was the "Basilica Apostolorum ad Catacumbas" (the basilica of the apostles at the catacombs). But what are the Catacombs? Is it Greek for sandpit? Which site first got the nickname and why did all the others adopt it? Indeed, some say that it was the name of a pub, "the Vessel" on the *Via Appia*, which served as a marker for local Christian cemeteries. St. Sebastian's is just over a mile down the *Appia*, and Christians, who were organized into legally recognized burial companies, owned the "Dormitories" as they called them, where their loved ones were briefly at rest, awaiting the Second Coming. Was it here that the great St. Jerome wandered below ground as a boy, and by the light of an oil lamp read the moving history of the early church in the epitaphs and graffiti?

I decide to look for an old favourite "Paule ed Petre, petite pro Victore" (Peter and Paul, pray for Victor) and I find it, but I had forgotten that this pilgrim Victor's prayer for patronage was only one of 12,000 petitions scratched on the red plaster wall. There must have been reasons for the fierce centring of prayer in such a place underground, along a Roman highway by which Paul travelled, even if Peter did not.

In honour of St. Sebastian, though probably to the puzzlement of the original saint himself, I recite Psalm 38: "Your arrows have sunk into me, your hand has come down on me". In the church above I see a set of footsteps, matching those in the chapel of Domine Quo Vadis, nearer the gate of Rome, said to be those of Christ as he stood and said to the fleeing Peter, "I am going to Rome to be crucified once more." I've seen such stones elsewhere in Italy associated with legends, but they are probably the recycled footprints of pagan gods who briefly touched base on earth. It is remarkable how many Catholics think the story comes from the Gospels, or at least from the Acts of the Apostles.

Looking neither right nor left, I go north the short distance to the city gate. And just in case the story be true, I am proud to be walking the last mile with Simon, most human of Apostles. In the shade of the Porta San Sebastiano I take leave of him, while he goes on north to the Tiber bank and to the Jewish quarter where he has friends, though there may be tension between the established community and the new Christian sect. The rest is martyrology.

My path is by Aurelian's Wall, built in vain in 271 A.D. against the menace of Barbarians. For centuries this was the limit of built-up Rome, though there was many an open space within. Most pilgrims saw Rome in ruins, with only baronial towers and church steeples as landmarks. I pause at the oratory of St. John-Boiled-In-Oil. I understand that it was not a fatal experience. Were all the apostles martyrs? Did John die of old age? Soon I can see the baptistery of St. John Lateran. The church is dedicated principally to our Saviour, but also to John the Baptist and John the Apostle. It is said that the Emperor Constantine, not long before he died, called in Pope Sylvester from his retreat on Mount Soracte and was baptised on this spot, which was land he had donated to the Church., thus giving the fag-end of a vicious, brutal and self-serving life to Christ, and ensuring the undying gratitude of the Church. The emperor, not Christ, was now the bridegroom of the Church.

My medieval guide-book tells me that there are to be seen here the Ark of the Covenant, the rods of Moses and Aaron, and the table of the Last Supper. It also warns women not to enter the chapel of St. John, though for men a plenary indulgence is on offer. Out of solidarity I refrain from entering that chapel, and so miss out on a picture of Christ when he was twelve years old.

Now I must concentrate on the object of my visit, the Confession and the medieval ciborium above it which is a reliquary for the silver-encased skulls of St. Peter and St. Paul. This church is the "Mater et caput Ecclesiarum" (mother and head of all churches) and the pope has his teaching chair (*Cathedra*) here, but it does not feature much on tourist itineraries nor sadly in the daily life of recent popes. At the Confession I read the longish Psalm 51, acknowledging my transgressions and asking for a new heart. Then I go East and stand before the last pillar. I look up at the last vestiges of a fresco commissioned of Giotto, Pope Boniface VIII proclaiming the first Jubilee.

It is February, and he stands on a balcony and the word goes out to all Christendom. Jerusalem once more is out of bounds, but the people can come to Rome, and they do in huge numbers. Was Dante amongst them? He speaks as though he was describing something he has seen.

Come I Roman per l'essercito molto
L'anno del gubileo su per lo ponte
hanno a passar la gente modo colto
che dal'un lato tutti hanno la fronte
verso 'l castello e vanno a santo Pietro
dal' altra sponda vanno verso 'l monte.

Inferno, XVIII, 29-32.

(The great crowd of Romans in the year of the Jubilee, as they cross the bridge, must pass in orderly fashion. On one side all face towards the castle and go towards St Peter's, on the other they go towards the hill)

In the first and only classic verse (in terza rima) in praise of a traffic control system, I wonder, by the way, if Dante is not thinking of Romei when he says Romans. The army of pilgrims for the jubilee were directed over the Ponte Sant' Angelo: those going to St. Peter's walked towards the Castel Sant' Angelo; those returning on the other side of the bridge walked towards 'the Jordan Mount' on the opposite river bank.

I go out into the square and the merciless sunshine to visit the Scala Santa. Pilgrims, as hardy as they are devout, go up the twenty-eight steps on their knees. Many a Pope and peasant has done the climb. But not I. I cannot bend the left knee, since a motor-bike accident ten years ago.

By stairs more comfortable I walk up to the Holy of Holies. At nine years' indulgence per stair, I realize I have missed out heavily, but I am consoled by the celebrated picture of Our Lord, Acheiropita (not painted by human hand) and venerated since the eighth century. I could wish that some human hand would remove the heavy incrustation of silver which hides most of it.

As I come out into the square again with its traffic islands and pedestrians risking life dodging between cars, I recall having read that once Philip Neri, a sixteenth-century saint, accepted a lift from a nobleman as he did the seven churches, but at St. John Lateran the rain was so heavy that the coach slid into the trench which had been formed by the workmen dragging an obelisk towards its present position near the church and palace. Horses, carriage and its occupants plunged into the deep hole. St. Philip clambered out smiling and went to a church nearby to pray. Oxen were summoned to drag out the horses. Everyone went home rejoicing. Diagonally across the traffic I make for the statue of St. Francis and companions. I wish St. Philip and St. Francis had met. Oh, what embracing and how much laughter there would have been. St. Dominic and St. Francis did meet, I think it was here, perhaps when Francis first came to seek papal approval for his rule. At first, Innocent III received him coolly, but that night the pope dreamt of St John Lateran, near collapse and being held up and saved from ruin by a barefoot friar.

The rule of St. Francis was eventually accepted by the next pope, a personal friend of the saint, but it was a hard battle, since it proposed a way of life which was dangerously close to the Gospels. Francis had a deep devotion to the Passion of Christ, and I think he was the first to bear the Stigmata. In the great days of Jubilee and pilgrimage, his spirituality inspired thousands, and will sustain me well enough, I hope, as I walk to Santa Croce in Gerusalemme.

This is not one of the four great basilicas, but makes the seven for the very good reason that for vast periods the Holy Land was not open to Christians, military or civilian. Thus Rome became the goal, and all the privileges and indulgences of the longer journey were transferred there.

Santa Croce already had its treasury, which even now, trimmed down and soberly arranged, is a witness to the fact that good Christians needed a sense of physical contact with the reality of the crucifixion. I find a corner in the Baroque church to recite my fifth Penitential Psalm: "I am like an owl of the wilderness, a lonely bird on the housetop" (Ps. 102). I love a really sad psalm, far more effective than repeating the same prayer over and over again, as pilgrims did to get the indulgence. I like a prayer to be one, and to have a beginning, a middle and an end. I think of the little child who went to confession and got three Hail Mary's as a penance. She burst into tears, "But I only know one Hail Mary" she said.

I'm ready to descend the stairs on the left and go below the altar to view the collection. The good and bad thief are named in the credits, but pride of place goes to the title over the cross in Hebrew, Greek and Latin: "Jesus of Nazareth, King of the Jews", the words Pilate insisted on.

Many of the relics here are said to have been found by Helena, mother of Constantine. Impossible to know if she really did bring a very large ship-load of memorabilia from Jerusalem.

Though it is delightful to think of Mary and Joseph saving up pieces of furniture from Bethlehem and Nazareth, in fact neither they nor the Christian community had any interest in such things. It is the mark of the middle-aged and the old to collect souvenirs. The first Christians were expecting the Last Judgement, if not today, at latest tomorrow. By the time the aged empress arrived, the Church had begun to acquire a taste for hoarding. The local merchants in Jerusalem saw her coming.

On a deeper level, it does disturb me that whereas the emphasis of the first Christians was on the resurrection, they never showed

Christ dead on the cross, yet in later centuries a morbid curiosity grew and a fascination with gory details of the suffering of Christ and the saints. I go out into the fresh air.

The route to St. Lawrence ought to be through countryside, but first I have to thread the iron and concrete maze of the approaches to the Termini Station as it cuts through the city wall. I look into the Campo Verano, Rome's major cemetery, once considered vast but now quite unable to contain all the dead who seek it. Now the maximum permitted space is three feet by two feet in a wall. This is done by downsizing the remains after they've been in the ground for a few years.

In Etruscan and Roman times cremations and burials went on side by side. The Church only reluctantly accepted cremation in the 1970s. I leave the Verano, turn the corner and I'm with St. Lawrence, one of the most popular martyrs. In Rome, for instance, I know of four more churches dedicated to him. He was a really kind deacon who cared for the poor, and bravely (even humorously, it is said) accepted martyrdom on a grid-iron over a slow fire.

His church, near the city gate, was on the itinerary from the earliest times. It had its own underground cemetery. In dangerous times, it was part of a little village, walled round against barbarians. I seek out the cloisters and recite psalm 130 as I walk round: "Out of the depths I cry to you O Lord".

On the fourth side of the marble-arcaded garden, I know I am going to be distracted by an inscription rescued from the catacombs below:

FLAVIA TIGRIS FILIA
CARISSIMA QUE VIXIT
ANNIS V MESES III DIES V, ORAS IIII

In the simplest Latin it says, "Flavia, dearest daughter of Tiger, who lived five years, three months, five days and four hours". It is the most moving funeral inscription I have ever read.

San Giminiano

Monteriggioni

Recumbent Bishop

IMAGO· ICONICA· BONIFACÍ · VIII· PONT · MAX·
IOBELAEVM· PRIMVM · IN· ANNVM· M·CCC· INDICENTIS·
PICTVRA· GIOTTI· AEQVALIS · EORVM · TEMPORVM·
QVAM· E· VETERI· PODIO· IN· CLAVSTRA· INDE· IN· TEMPLVM · TRANSLATAM·
GENS·CAIETANA · NE· AVITVM· MONVMENTVM·VETVSTATE· DELERETVR·
ANNO · M· DCC·LXXXVI· CRYSTALLO · OBTEGENDAM·CVRAVIT

The Jubilee proclaimed

St Francis arrives in Rome

Jonah and the Sea-monster

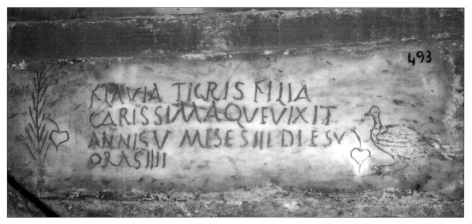

Flavia daughter of Tiger

The Arch of Trajan, Benevento

Roman Road, Egnatia

Brindisi: the two columns

Inside the church, after privately reciting Vespers, I sit quietly and remember that this was the favourite church of Pius IX. He had started as a vaguely liberal pope and had even chosen a Prime Minister, and taken tentative steps towards a democracy of sorts, but Rossi was assassinated and Pius IX was traumatized. Rome was seized by the new Italian army and Pius became the Prisoner in the Vatican. After a long and conservative reign he died, and at midnight on July 12th, 1878, his body was taken from the Vatican Palace surrounded by loyal young Catholics.

But youthful revolutionaries ambushed the cortege at the Ponte Sant' Angelo and almost threw the coffin into the Tiber. With great difficulty his body was brought to San Lorenzo and is now encased in marble high up in the apse.

I've digressed. These are supposed to be short business-like, vow-fulfilling visits, so I must make straight for St. Mary Major. On the way I resist the temptation of such delightful diversions as the capuchins on the Via Veneto, whose crypt chapels contain the bones of friars arranged most tastefully as high relief ceiling decoration, though some bones remain connected and they lean out of alcoves as fully assembled brown-habited Capuchins.

But St. Mary Major calls this pilgrim to complete the seven churches as promised, and I walk rather tired up the large apron of steps. I'm on the last stretch. It is like a homecoming.

The church, though it has grown grand over the years, has kept such things as its picture-post-card mosaics of the life of Mary, around the walls, and has a glorious mosaic in the apse, needlessly obscured by the massive baldacchino.

Down the steps into the Confession. Here some wood from the very manger of Bethlehem has been preserved. Today I have accomplished a little thing, and if I have looked askance at anything, then I make one with the psalmist who said, "Lord, do not enter into judgement with your servant, for no-one is righteous before you". I've almost fulfilled this day's vow, and there is a community of the English College for communion and a choice of three religious

129

communities for confessor. Now I can give myself a little bonus, go down a side street and visit Santa Prassede.

This Roman lady welcomed local Christians into her house. Her courtyard remains and inside the main door of the church is a statue of Santa Prassede sponging up the blood of the martyrs and squeezing it into a pot.

There is also a gem of a ninth-century chapel, once popularly called the Garden of Paradise, more properly the chapel of St. Zeno, covered with mosaics. Amongst the saints, but with the square nimbus of the living, is Theodora Episcopa. Theodora what? Don't tell that to the opponents of women's ordination. I re-enter the church and pick up a chair to sit at the feet of a pilgrim who made it to Rome, but died here. The flat, polished, marble floor-tomb shows a merchant pilgrim with a large hat, a shell, a bag and a large stick with a point. Round the edge in Latin is the inscription "This is the tomb of John of Montopoli, merchant. What I was, you are. What I am, you will be. Pray for me a sinner. Do Penance". Sad, but at least he reached his goal.

Now I could complete the circle by going down to the Trevi Fountain, and follow the ancient custom of throwing a coin in the hope of returning but I give it a miss and go through the narrow streets to the all-holy Pantheon, beneath whose floor are countless bones of Christians brought from the catacombs for fear of the Saracens. On through the stadium of Domitian now the Piazza Navona to seek the Ponte Sant' Angelo, the bridge of which Dante spoke, and I think of another Holy Year, 1450, when a dense crowd of pilgrims was crossing the bridge and some horses took fright. Many pilgrims were trampled underfoot, others fell into the Tiber, several hundred died. Two memorial chapels were erected at the entrance to the bridge, but since anti-papal parties later used them as a base to attack the pope's stronghold across the water, they were considered to be desecrated and were demolished and replaced in 1527 by statues of St. Peter and St. Paul.

From the left bank, I look up at the Tomb of Hadrian, the

massive red-brick core, once marble-clad and topped with pine-trees. Deep inside they have preserved the words of that pagan philosopher and good emperor: a message to his own soul.

ANIMULA VAGULA BLANDULA
HOSPES COMESQUE CORPORIS
QUAE NUNC ABIBIS IN LOCA
PALLIDULA RIGIDA NUDULA
NEC UT SOLES DABIS JOCOS

(Poor little harmless little soul
guest and companion of the body
whither do you go now
pale, terrified, shiftless little one
bereft even of your gentle pleasantries?}

No wonder Pope Gregory the Great wished to make Hadrian an honorary Christian. Facing the Castel Sant' Angelo I work out the directions given by Dante to pilgrims 600 years ago.

I go a few steps further, lean on the parapet, and take in the classic view, the outline of St. Peter's against the western sky. It tells me that today's little journey is ended.

There remains for me only the civilised company of The English College.

A Papal Audience

There are some who have a private audience with the pope, others attend as part of a group. But anyone can turn up for the Angelus led by the pope. It's the easiest way to see him, if you don't mind sharing.

So here I am in good time, and I go to the side of the square furthest from the Papal Palace, and sit on the base of a Bernini Column. It is nearly midday. His window is open, with a bit of carpet hanging over the sill. The midday Angelus led by the Pope has recently become very popular and most people think it dates from apostolic times. Not by about 1900 years. I am resting, doing no harm to anyone, when suddenly my sunlight is blocked by two smartly-dressed fully-armed policemen, hotfoot from a Gilbert and Sullivan comic opera.

"Non si puo stare seduto" (Literally "You can't stand seated here") a pompous way of saying "Stand up for the pope". I decide to play along: "O, che senso di potere!" I reply ("what a kick it must give you to say that!"). "But Colonel," I ask obsequiously, "is it only now that I must not stand seated, or is it on Monday also, or only where there is a full moon?"

By now a little crowd has gathered, and the boss-man, discomforted turns suddenly and points skywards, "Ecco il Papa!" (Look, the Pope) which is a lie, but while everyone turns to look up at a Pope who is not there, the two pantomime figures march off to pester some other pilgrim. Fully seven minutes later a curtain twitches, a microphone crackles, and the pope is steered to the window. In a clear voice he leads the Angelus. The courage of the man! He then begins a little talk, which seems to echo the Gospel of the day. Even his desire to speak to us is a message. But his voice begins to fade and he ends with a gesture which we take as a blessing. A woman near me says, "He's saying goodbye", and her friend is crying. I am moved, but am I the only person in the whole world who would like the brave man to retire?

I shall spend my last day in Rome in the company of Abbot Nikulaus, poet and pilgrim. His interest in all he saw was no mere curiosity. Each day he dictated a brief account to his secretary of the churches and monuments he had seen, and he left us with a concise twelfth-century guide book. Ancient Rome, by his estimate was four miles in length and two miles in breadth. I have walked the whole twelve-mile circuit of the Aurelian walls several times, and at a guess I would say he is right.

I join him in St. John Lateran, which, as he points out, is the only church with a bishop's throne, though there are substitute chairs for the Bishop of Rome kept at St. Mary Major and St. Lawrence, should he wish to speak as bishop when he visits them. Nikulaus quotes without comment the claim that St. John's has a garment of Mary and some of her silk, also the foreskin of Christ and a great part of the Crown of Thorns. He tells me something I would not have known: St. Agnese, well outside the walls on the *Via Nomentana*, is by far the most splendid church he has seen. Who now visits this distant, half-ruined church on which Constantine ostentatiously lavished great imperial wealth ? The abbot speaks of what he saw, and in his time St. Lawrence and St. Agnes had no rivals. With Nikulaus as guide, and at a brisk pace, we go west from the Lateran. He points out the equestrian statue of the sainted Constantine. I dare not mention it, but it is really that of the good pagan Marcus Aurelius. If the people had known it they would have destroyed it, horse and all, instead of worshipping it here, until the day when it was moved to the distant Capitoline. We pass ruins, pagan and Christian, and, before my eyes, outlines of buildings appear, dissolve and reappear according to their fate in history.

Christianity was never a totally underground religion, *pace* Wiseman and Fabiola, and it began to live and breathe the free air of Rome on the Coelian hill. indeed, with members of the imperial family converting, it gradually became the IN religion. Churches were built on the ruins of Mithraic temples.

These musings have taken us to the Campus Martius, almost to the Tiber. Our way has been signposted by the campanili which began to spring up at the time of the abbot's journey to Rome. The name of these bell towers came from the "Campagna", or more precisely from Nola on the slopes of Vesuvius.

What a brilliantly simple idea, a tall, slender, highly visible tower pierced with arches at the top, with a bell to summon the faithful.

As we enter the Pantheon, I refrain from calling it "Santa Maria ad martyres" and hear Nikulaus call it instead "the church of All

Saints". "It is open above", he says, a simple description of the unique dome. As we look up through it to the sky, the nine centuries which separate us are as nothing.

We go on across the Tiber to St. Peter's, which he calls "very large and splendid" and tells me that "here there is full absolution from the perplexities of men the wide world over". He remarks that we are entering the church from the east. The prevailing tradition used to be to enter from the west. In all my years I had not noticed this detail of the alignment of St. Peter's. He notes that Constantine placed the altar centrally and that the sarcophagus of St. Peter is directly below. This fact was always known by pilgrims as being significant. As I kneel with him at the Confessional, I close my eyes and I am momentarily overwhelmed by the joyful thought that the Church of Bramante, Michelangelo and (God preserve us) Sangallo is after all nothing but a bad dream.

Abbot Nikulaus is now in his element, walking here and there, taking measurements. He knows that the exact placement of the church is crucial. I do not even protest when he makes me pace out the length and breadth of the Basilica of Constantine. I've measured it from side to side. It is 460 feet long and 230 feet wide. We go outside to find the obelisk which once stood in the stadium where Peter died, possibly the last thing on earth the martyr saw. (Bernini later moved it from the side of St. Peter's to the square so the Pope could see it from his window, like a garden gnomon).

The abbot asks me if I have done "The Five Churches" and I realise that in his day Santa Croce and St. Sebastian were probably out of fashion.

What a privilege to be, even for a time, and across the ages, a soul-mate of this great but modest man. Before we part he says to me, almost by the way, "No one is so wise as to know all the churches in the city of Rome."

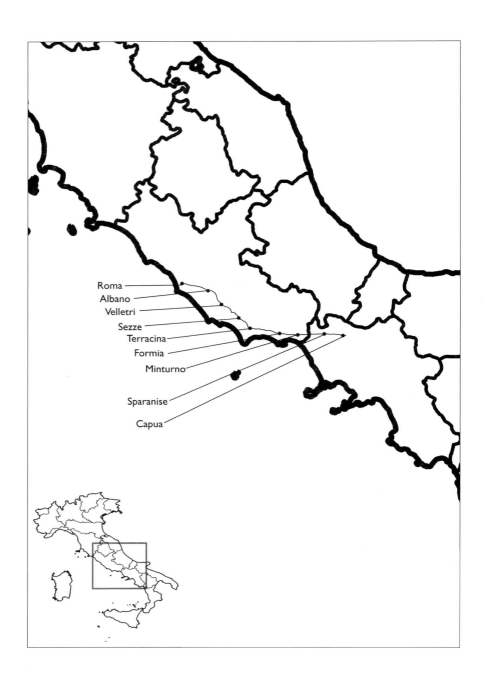

Roma
Albano
Velletri
Sezze
Terracina
Formia
Minturno
Sparanise
Capua

Rome to Capua: 10th July-22nd July

For most pilgrims Rome was a goal, and more than sufficient. They went no further, they turned for home. Belloc, who made straighter for Rome than ever any other pilgrim did, entered by the Flaminian gate, and while waiting twenty minutes for Mass glanced at an Egyptian obelisk, had bread and brandy at a café on the Corso, and his vow was fulfilled..

With others there lingered the desire, not only to see Rome but also to visit the Holy Land and trace the Saviour's footsteps, but so rich were the rewards offered at Rome's substitute shrines, and so many were the relics of the Passion housed in Rome, that it seemed a long and dangerous way to trace, for little gain. South of Rome, Italy has never been safe, until the twentieth century.

Even the nineteenth-century English travellers tell us of bandits hanging from gibbets at the crossroads. And even if medieval pilgrims reached the ports of Apulia, they would need to find a place on a boat, merchant or military, to take them to Greece or the Levant.

Then, as now, the Holy Land was never at peace, and rarely safe. The crusades offered some hope of safety but can anyone name a crusade which was successful or did not leave the situation worse than before? Christ might just possibly have had something to say on the subject, had any of his followers been listening.

For most pilgrims the short journey down the *Appia* to the southern catacombs was as near as they came to Jerusalem. Did they look down the road built by the blind counsul which ran 400 miles to Bari, and did they reluctantly turn on their heel, as at the turning point of a Roman Stadium? (That of Maxentius lay in ruins nearby.)

Not so the intrepid Nikulaus of Munkatvera. Having made it thus far from Iceland he now took the opportunity to visit Campania, as we shall see.

Today I am in the heart of Rome. I have spent more than a month either in community, or visiting friends or using modern means to revisit parts of my recent journey.

I stand by the Meta Sudans (the sweating milestone) hard by the Colosseum where once the gladiators performed ritual ablutions before entering the arena and I walk straight through the arch of Constantine, whose only worthwhile carvings are those stolen from Trajan. On past the tip of the Circus Maximus, where more martyrs suffered than ever did in the Colosseum, out through the original boundary of the city and down the narrow tombland of the pagans where the ashes of the Scipios are pigeon-holed in their Columbaria.

Nikulaus speaks high praise of the upper route through Frascati, Ferentino and Benedictine Monte Cassino on to Capua. His argument is that it is free from the Mal Aria of the plains. I have not the heart to tell him that Mussolini drained the Pontine Marshes, as I choose to take the *Appia Antica*. Hearing this, the Abbot Nikolaus reels off the names of places on my route, as though he knew them well. "Be sure to mark the 40th milestone, where Christians came out to meet citizen Paul as he came under military escort to endure house arrest in Rome. There is nearby a posting station with the popular name 'the three inns" he adds hopefully. As we part I wish I knew how to say "Goodbye, God Bless" in twelfth-century Icelandic.

The first few miles of the Appia are very familiar territory, no need to explore; a simple nod in the direction of ruined tombs will do. Here the foot traveller has to be nimble and wary. Cars rattle along unaware of anything but themselves. Today I can spare no more than a reverence towards the catacombs. The road passes over the cemeteries, I am walking over the bones of the first Christians. Mind you, wherever you go these days you are walking on bones. After a couple of miles, the road is officially barred to traffic, which practically halves the number of cars using it.

As I draw near to Ciampino Airport to the east, I can see the new Appian road teeming with driven people, who do not know how to saunter. But now I am becoming quite uneasy. The tombs have become the haunt of unsavoury characters who loiter there waiting for the cars which bump along the Roman flagstones.

Others sit in groups in the marble seat circles where once noble roman families met to honour their dead. Shabby and listless, they look vaguely across at me from under hooded eyelids. I walk on quickly, and the Appia crosses the busy south circular. A signpost points to a famous sanctuary of Our Lady. Suddenly from this point I am once more a lone traveller on the road to Beneventum.

About 300 BC the blind Censor Appius Claudius recognized that Roman conquest and Roman business would need a road deep into "Greater Greece", the far south of what we now call Italy. Since his day the Via Appia has been modified, added to and improved in many ways, but this is the road to begin all roads. We are now at the foot of the Alban hills and the road climbs above the plain. Below us straight lines make up a web of roads, canals, fences, trees, filling the flatland between us and the sea.

Albano is hardly important, but it is one of many resorts where the rich and the moderately comfortable escape from Rome. The Christian will not be surprised if here churches, such as St. Peter's were built on the ruins of pagan temples or baths. The campanile of that church was built from material rescued from ruins. There is even a pagan inscription carefully turned upside-down. Was this intentional, in the way that pagan capitals were used as bases for Christian columns? I'm here in broad daylight, but I seek out the church of Santa Maria della Rotonda because here somewhere between the hours of nine and ten on the night of November 23rd 1848, Fr. Liebl waited in the shadows for a coach coming post haste from Rome. Out stepped a rotund priest fearful and wearing dark glasses, all the while his companions reassuring him, in thick Bavarian accents, "Holy Father, no one will recognise you in the guise of an ordinary priest". Pio Nono was fleeing towards the kingdom of Naples. Only a week ago his palace on the Quirinal had been bombarded by troops of the Risorgimento. His Latin Secretary had been shot dead at a window by a sniper. A month before this the pope had declined the offer of safe conduct to France from a French bishop, saying melodramatically, "I might meet Christ returning to Rome to be crucified".

Pius was not the only pope to go back and forth on this road. For centuries they commuted between such places as Anagni or the other possessions of the Gaetani, and Orsini and Conti di Segni families. Many of them spent very little time indeed in Rome.

Although I've done only fourteen miles, I shall not diverge to go the two miles to Castel Gandolfo, popular since the 1950s with pilgrims who go to summer audiences with the pope. I could be tempted by the thought of the lake, and the view of the English College Palazzola, but the heat has weakened me and I have a tough journey tomorrow.

From Albano, St. Paul looking north will have had his first view of Rome: plenty of marble to catch the sun. Rome, exactly as Augustus had left it; Rome before Nero reduced it to ashes. But I am going south and the road brings me quickly to Ariccia, unimportant as always, and a disappointment to Horace, that most likeable of poets, friend of the rich but no friend of healthy exercise. He stayed at a very modest hotel, nothing like the villas of his patrons. He was on a diplomatic mission on the way to Brundisium, but found plenty to amuse himself, mainly the disasters of the journey. No doubt we'll meet up with him and them.

Genzano does not attract me, though once a year it is crowded with pilgrims and onlookers. The main street is carpeted with flowers for the feast of Corpus Domini. I remember in the '60s being in the crowd as the procession with the Blessed Sacrament made its way up to the church. A student pointed out a socialist party banner floating proudly amongst the others. "They wouldn't be seen dead in church though", said a local. Shades of Don Camillo.

(Habitarunt di quoque silvas (The gods live in these woods), Virgil, *Eclogues*, 2.60)

It is lake Nemi just below the town which draws me. Minuscule, wooded and gloomy. I love it, and over the years I've spent many hours there, alone and not alone. Here, if anywhere, one can believe in the survival of that endangered species, the ancient pagan gods.

Sir James Frazer, esteemed and ground-breaking anthropologist, found inspiration here for his imaginative scientific book *The Golden Bough*. He ranges widely through magic and religion, dealing with tree-spirits and reciting tales of gods and goddesses, using the lake as a starting point but drawing examples from every age and continent . But how much are we to trust him?

Judge for yourself when he tells us what "Gascon peasants believe about the Mass of Saint Secaire; how very few priests know this Mass and three-fourths of those who know it would not say it for love or money". He has wicked priests performing the gruesome ceremony, and absolution is reserved to the Pope of Rome alone.

The setting must be in a ruined church where owls mope and hoot, and bats flit in the gloaming and where toads squat under the desecrated altar. The Mass is mumbled backwards and ends just as the clocks are knelling the midnight hour.

I forebear to relate the worst of this arrant tosh. I suppose his excuse is that he is only quoting peasants.

And yet, all alone in these woods, even a scientist might believe just anything.

I could have turned down to Lanuvium, following the original pre-Christian road, but I shall keep up higher, travelling between vines to Velletri where pilgrims and Popes felt safer from the invasions of Barbarians and malaria.

One or other of its churches will surely have been built on the ruins of a pagan temple and they are dedicated to saints popular with pilgrims: Lawrence, Martin, Peter.

The railway station just outside the town, besides being most pleasantly marbled, has an inscription which praises Pope Pius IX in glowing terms, for in his early days he was both liberal and modern. His predecessor, Gregory XVI, had called the railway "the stinking agent of the devil", but Pius brought the iron road to Velletri and the citizens have never forgotten the favour.

The road down into the plain is almost straight. By tomorrow I know that there will not be a kink or curve in sight. I can find no trace of the Forum Appii, though it was important in its day and known to St. Paul

I have with me a satire by Horace, and try to place the action of his hastily scribbled account. Whereas tonight I know I shall sleep soundly and comfortably, Horace was at this point having terrible trouble with slaves, innkeepers and boatmen. As the evening draws on, I am in danger of becoming bored, not a croaking frog to disturb me, not a single 'cursed mosquito' (*Mali culices*).

Horace of course was not walking; he had chosen to make a night-trip by barge along the canal which keeps pace with the *Appia*. But the boatman tied up the craft and skived off, and little progress was made. I'm better off on foot.

Minus est gravis Appia tardis

(The Via Appia is less taxing for those who go slowly)
(Horace, *Satires, I.5.*)

Yes, Horace, dear Roman friend, but you had Heliodorus, the most learned of all Greeks, for company, and you had slaves to swear at, and vile water to give you the runs. I'm on my own (the water I filter and boil for safety's sake).

The cicadas resonate under the umbrella pines. This road (the longest straight stretch in Italy) is such that all straight lines should be measured against it. But there is a limit to the satisfaction given by the sight of these trees shimmering as they make a bee-line for vanishing point. I am driven to find interest in names such as Epittafio – 'Inscription'. Not even the tomb of a hero, I learn, but merely words of praise for another attempt to drain the marshes. For this is the Pontine, the bridge between Rome and Naples. Several popes tried to get rid of the stagnant waters, and where they could not they built bridges to cross the fens on stilts, but they were no more successful than Caesar of old. People scurried along the road by day and turned to the hill towns by night.

At the cross-roads for Sezze I do likewise, but not before I have asked the café owner the names of the local canals. "The higher, the middle and the lower ditch," says he. Ask a daft question. Though there is a ditch named after Pope Pius VI who had it excavated, and another after Pope Sixtus V who repressed brigandage.

Thursday 17th July I take the bus down to the cross-roads. No one has moved the stones I set down last night and soon I am a mile down the road, a solitary dot on a line which points to infinity. The map names this stretch 'storta' (twisted), I am glad to see cartographers have a sense of humour.

There are Roman ruins and the remains of a tower - at least living beings once dwelt here.

By mid-afternoon I'm tired, not from the distance but from the relentless heat. In the evening Anxur and the Temple of Jupiter come into sight, but I cannot judge the distance and I read the signs that I am not particularly well.

Dull backache, unwarranted tiredness, but above all irritable-soul syndrome are sure signs that I have kidney problems.

Horace, after an unsatisfactory night-journey, crawled his way after breakfast three miles up to the hill to Anxur perched on her far gleaming rocks. At the end of the day I do the same.

Half-way up the headland there is a plateau on which stood the city. Horace, tired and with a headache, dragged his feet to the capitol and bowed to Jupiter, Juno and Minerva, each provided with a temple, no doubt begun by local tribes such as the Aurunci and the Volsci, but embellished by the new empire. There is not the slightest doubt that the flagstones which are now revealed (courtesy of friendly allied bombing in 1943) are those which bruised the tired feet of Horatius Flaccus. Next, as he struggled on, he cannot have failed to see the building works and the large flight of steps leading to a temple newly dedicated to Augustus his master.

The new regime valued the support of immensely rich patrons such as Maecenas who not only funded projects, but also used poets as publicists for the brave new age which was dawning in the generation before Christ was born. The easy-going Horace enjoyed the luxuries showered on him whilst sublime souls such as Virgil scaled the heights. "Tu regere imperio populos Romane memento …parcere subjectis et debellare superbos" (Oh Roman, remember to rule with authority, to spare those you conquer and crush those who defy you).

At last the hilltop, and the pre-Roman, vast, porticoed Temple of Jupiter Anxur. The setting sun reveals the Pontine Islands. There are times when even Vesuvius is visible to the south, but not today.

Down to the port, and lodgings. Down to earth also, as I think through a serious problem. I am not fit to go on. It is ridiculous, even considering the heat, that I am so tired, and even confused.

Since leaving Rome I've taken far too long to walk to Terracina, sixty miles in four days. Why not say to myself, "You've walked from the Gran San Bernado to Rome. Let that be your journey. Count anything else as extra."

I'll stop here awhile and make a decision in a few days. But I do want to walk the *Appia*. I do want to get to Brindisi, and there make an end of my tale and my journey.

Is it Horace who whispers once more in my ear that the road is more agreeable if you take it easy?

Friday 18th July. Here Horace put black ointment on his sore eyes, and made rendezvous with Maecenas, Cocceius and Capito who were on an important diplomatic mission to Brindisi. He had friends who would share a joke and listen to his complaints as they journeyed south. At this moment I could do with a companion on my journey I may have to abandon the exercise but, *Carpe Diem* (Make the most of each day), I'll look around Terracina with the fascinating medieval Duomo mushrooming out of the mulch of a pagan Roman temple.

Already, for the Romans, the town was shrouded in mystery; vague stories of Spartan exiles, Etruscan memories too, and local tribes with their own folklore. The Volscians had a god called Anxur who still clings to the headland by his fingertips, but of him remains only the name. This mountain has always had a sacred dedication, I do not know which Christian warrior tribe, Byzantine, Lombard or Norman, dedicated it to St. Michael the Archangel.

My main purpose today is to visit the church of St. Cesario. The bishop's church would in the Greek south always have been called the cathedral, from its teaching chair, but in many places the alternative name 'Duomo' is used. The 'House' is the house of God and home of the people. I could sit forever in the square which was once the Forum, and look across to the steep steps upon which pagans too had gazed 2000 years ago. How far they were allowed to penetrate into the arcane 'Fanum' (most sacred spot) beyond, I do not know, or whether they were allowed to shelter under the arcade with its columns crowned by Corinthian capitals. My attention is all on the Christian decoration along the architrave: eagles, falcons and every kind of animal, both real and monstrous. I realise that any pagan would feel at home with them, as also with the soldiers who stand on either side of their mystic standard cross.

I have the right, as every Christian has, to enter our own house, and this I do, coming into my own. This house is a basilica, a royal residence. A carpet of finely-composed marble fragments leads to a raised area fit for a judge to be enthroned there, but modified to seat the clergy and house an altar.

The space I am in (the nave) would for many centuries have been an organic whole, a living space for people, not cut across by benches like a sliced loaf. Here people met and mingled and were one. They could gather beneath the marvelous high pulpit to be fed by the word and then bodily turn toward the sanctuary to be nourished at the table of the Lord. On the altar steps is a Pascal Candle, carved and signed, Sicilian-Norman and proud of it. This temple knows the God that dwells within, and to its initiates it tells its tale.

There are other churches of mild interest in this town, but I have seen them before, and need to husband my energies and to make for the topmost temple of the headland.

I am on the road which for five centuries ploughed relentlessly across the brow of the hill and descended south into the marshes.

The great god Jupiter Anxur could look down the coastline to Vesuvius or out to sea and the Pontine Islands, mere rocks with scarcely a tree clinging to them. Until recently they were used to house criminals and political exiles. Now they attract tourists.

The pagan ruins, if not beautiful are considerable, and I take refuge from the sun under the long arcaded cryptoporticus and watch the lazy life of the harbour below. It has never been a busy port, for it has no hinterland to serve. There is a small livelihood for local fishermen, and a few small boats cross regularly to the islands. I walk slowly down in the cool of the evening to my hotel. I suppose it is time for me to make a decision, but I don't.

Saturday 19th July. Yesterday was just right; picking the bones of Roman pagan temples and allowing the imagination to run riot in one of the best medieval churches on the route. But I know I owed a lot to pain killers, and I mustn't let them cloud my judgment. So it is day by day for the moment. Formia, just ahead, will be a good base. I shall put my kidney passport, complete with photos, in my pocket, and do ten miles or so a day.

Today I shall footle gently round the headland to San Biagio, courtesy of the blessed Emperor Trajan who shaved the cliff as one shaves parmesan cheese, and built a road round it at sea level, thus saving the weary traveller the task of hiking over the top. No wonder he is an honorary Christian, and is forgiven a few martyrdoms. Trajan may not have foreseen the abuse of his road by modern drivers who try to cut corners and think that pedestrians are fair game to be terrorised.

His contemporary, Juvenal, complained bitterly about "fourwheelers cutting corners" (redarum transitus arto vicorum in flexu). Once I've survived the curve and the road ahead is straight, I go and lean on a wall and look seaward, for the *Appia* angles inland. Formerly this was to avoid a large shallow lagoon. All that is left today is the small lake of Fondi. I'm now crossing the plain of Fondi, past the site of one Custom House, where, until the nineteenth century, a merchant would have had to pay dues and a pilgrim would have had to claim poverty as well as piety. After a gap there is another customs post, and watch-tower standing nearby like an exclamation-mark..

This has always been border country, though under the present cartography we are a fair hike from the Lazio-Campania border. A tree-shaded avenue preceded the climb to the safety and shelter of the hill-top town 400 feet above. In the heat I find it hard going, but for many years I have never approached a hill-top town for the first time, except on foot. At the very first shop on the outskirts of San Biagio I buy and gulp down a large bottle of mineral water, and seek the shade of the Church of St. John the Baptist.

In its wall is a reused Appian road milestone. They measured in honest miles in those days, not in new-fangled kilometers. As I lean on a wall and look west (the whole village is like a balcony). I ask two locals about their Roman past. They point to ruins on the downward slope, the work of Caracalla, who is fulsomely praised in local lore (as is not uncommon with mad tyrants). But let us praise good men. St. Blaise is honoured here (and all along the pilgrim way). He is said to have been an Armenian, probably martyred by Licinius, rival emperor to Constantine. By the eighth century he was established as a healer of animals and humans, being particularly effective for illness of the throat. On February 3rd, his feast, supplicants are touched with candles newly blest at Candlemas as a specific against all illness of throat and voice. Pilgrims have no special immunity, and as every traveller knows the most common ailment caught abroad is a sore throat. The second is diarrhoea, but I know of no saint with special powers to cure the latter.

Sunday 20th July I go to the church of John the Baptist in San Biagio. The people in their church, singing well and led by teenagers are at one with the Christ whom pilgrims seek. They are also linked to the pilgrims to whom they have offered hospitality over the centuries.

I feel I have made a good start and I'm prepared to do far more than a Sabbath journey. Well, to Formia at least. Down below I find my five stones still there (but somewhat scattered) and make a start.

The first stretch is flat, though not long enough to be boring and it gets me to Fondi., the apex of a triangle, for here the road angles back to the sea. Ahead of me is a minor pass and the magical Monte Cristo overhanging Gaeta.

Fondi is reassuring. It has a Porta Romana, and a tiny Roman centre on a grid plan. Horace laughed at its self-important Praetor, Aufidius Luscus, who had been a little fish when in Rome, but now was proud to come out with all the trimmings in public procession to meet great Maecenas ("A friend of mine you know"). What a disparate group, this travelling circus described by Horace; vastly wealthy Maecenas, patron of the arts, who also

148

bankrolled imperial projects: Horace who was there to provide the humour, even if he did disgrace himself by admitting he had fled the battlefield of Actium, leaving his shield behind. There were others in the caravan, even great Virgil who could, with his inspired poetry help sell the New Empire to the masses.

Unassuming little Fundi has always quietly prospered.

It deserves its peaceful, deeply moving twelfth-century crucifix and Cosmatesque marble work (brought all the way from the Roman workshops of the Cosmati family).

Itri is next, but what a vision of woe! It is like coming upon an accident. I had no warning. Anything old has been destroyed. To reach the medieval city I must climb the narrow steps hemmed in by crumbling houses, not all of them rebuilt since the friendly bombing of the last war. How vulnerable is everything that is civilised. Ancient arches lean over as if they wished to comfort me. But I will not be comforted.

Stone for stone, picture for picture, the invasions of barbarians and all the natural cataclysms through the ages have not destroyed half as much of Italy's heritage as did the liberation of Italy by its allies in 1943-44.

In the medieval quarter, two old churches stand, with remains of the Byzantine, Norman and Gothic, but they are derelict. Desolate, I go down to the road again and head for Formia, which will serve me for a resting place. Since I do not wish to dwell on the thought of churches as collateral damage (the "Oops, sorry" syndrome), I'll chase one sad thought out with another. I am within a lazy evening's walk of Formia where Cicero had a villa. This great orator, and courageous upholder of what passed for democracy in his day, hated the vile opportunist Mark Anthony, and wrote two diatribes against him, and thus sealed his own fate.

I've studied the road, and made some enquiries, and wish to do the last two or three miles not on tarmac but on the rough-surfaced path which crosses the harsh dunes, and descends to the coast and to Formia. As I stoop to touch a rugged plant, rooted in a gritty soil (broom or gorse, I do not know), I am startled to hear the sound of rushing chariot wheels and I recognise the old man in sweat-stained toga as he rushes past me, fear in his staring eyes, seeking his villa and safety. But I am helpless to break his fate, and it is not long before two huge chariots manned by thugs fill the air with dust and curses. If only I could have sent them by a wrong track and saved the old man who spoke of peace as "tranquil liberty" and of servitude as "the worst of all evils". But these murderers did not even see me. It was as though I did not exist. I still have Cicero in mind as I halt in the tall shadow of a monument and sepulchre named for him on the outskirts of the town.

In Formia I seek advice. The chemist looks at the remaining painkillers nestling in my hot little hand, and raises his eyebrows. Then he issues, more of the same.

"Rest", I tell myself, pacing up and down, and I go to spend an hour or two in the town's excellent little museum, and to chase up a reference in a letter of Cicero to Atticus, in which he refused the gift of a painting or Ares, god of War, on the grounds that he, Marcus Tullius, was a pacifist. In theory he was, but tell that to the shades of Catiline and his fellow-conspirators. Cicero considered them a danger to his beloved republic and condemned them to death, giving them no right of appeal. This he did "republicae causa" (for the public good) and not for personal gain. It is good to know that you are being executed for the best possible motives. Politics and governance have never been anything else but nasty. Do not believe those who would seek to tell you otherwise. They are either fools or knaves.

For a brief days rest now as a diversion I shall cross to the Pontine Islands, whose mournful rocks have been watered by the salt tears of political exiles from every period of Roman and Italian history. Here the local people scratch a modest living from its meagre soil, or farm the seas for fish or welcome tourists.

I'm fit enough now, I'm sure, to walk the *Via Appia*, perhaps as far as Capua, and then I shall take a very necessary break and visit a monastery and friends in Calabria. Ahead is a relatively new section of the road, built in Trajan's time. As I walk along I find that I am part of a mini-drama. The people have gathered on the sea-shore. All are standing. They are not looking out to sea, but inland, whence a droning sound is heard, increasingly loud, as two chunky little yellow planes appear from the east. As they cross the shore line they lower one wing, and the crowd pirouette, as under the baton of a chorus master. The planes run north along the coast. By now all eyes are looking west, and we watch the planes descend to water level, skimming the surface and scooping up water. They struggle to rise, and turn inland almost within touching distance of our heads, or so it seems. Some people even crouch as they turn to watch them go inland.

Ponderously the planes make for the hills in the middle distance where little mushroom clouds of smoke hang over the forests. I can't see them winning the battle

On the open road once more, with temperatures in the mid-thirties Celsius, there is also smoke trapped in the heat haze, and there is the pleasant sickly sweet taste of pine-resin burning like incense. Patches of scrub and stubble are alight, but neither I nor anyone feels any sense of urgency or that we are in danger.

But I am angry. Yes. I rage and shake my fist at a car which has just passed me on the road going south. The occupant has thrown a cigarette end, still alight, onto the tinder-dry grass verge.

It seems to me that these cigarette smokers are like badly brought up four-year-olds. These idiots cannot take on the proposition that actions have consequences. (I think the kidney stones perhaps are talking here.)

Minturno beckons from a steep hill to the left. It is a pilgrim stop, but for me the main interest is Thomas Aquinas, theologian and celebrity after-dinner speaker, who was in great demand throughout fourteenth-century Christendom at gatherings of Bishops and the like.

Minturno was his bolt-hole because here, not far from his native Aquinum he could always take a break at the castle. His sister

Adelasia (surely a Lombard name?) was the wife of Count Roger (surely a Norman?) who owned the Castle of Minturno.

Safe from contemporary paparazzi he could take his ease. The grateful town has carved a perpetual memorial of his holiday visit in the summer of 1272.

Minturno has more to offer than its castle. The cathedral has a pulpit to be proud of and a wall sculpture of Jonah and the sea monster.

In several churches near here (Gaeta cathedral is one) the story of Jonah is told. Medieval pilgrims expected to come across the story of Jonah, this reluctant "Christian". Christ, when he was preaching, could confidently talk of the accident-prone prophet, when he wished to sow the seed of understanding about his own death and resurrection. Sadly these days Jonah is only found in pub-quizzes, where you are expected to remember a whale connection.

Worse than that, Christians, like most people today perhaps, have lost all sense of metaphor, allegory or parable. Nor do we grasp the purpose of art, which is to tell our story, rather than to put us to sleep. Most people would be ill at ease if they were asked to apply their mind to a picture or a parable.

The vibrant carvings of the middle ages no longer have power to move. Our churches are degraded by mass-produced low-grade repetitions of the banal.

When were you last challenged by a holy picture?

Leaving the Roman town of Minturnae and setting off along the Appia I'm about to turn inland, going east and south. On this pilgrimage I shall not see the Tyrrhenian sea again. I do not intend to lose touch with Horace and his friends who met for a party here: "O qui complexus et gaudia quanta fuerunt" (Oh what embracing and what joy there was!). They must be somewhere near, I can hear the glad cries, the back-slapping and the laughter. Nor can I renounce my interest in the pagan world around. We presume that pilgrims ignored everything pagan. I think they absorbed much more than has been admitted, and transformed the most exciting bits into popular legends. (But I can check that with medieval companions further down the road.) This border country was once malarial, and was always exposed to pirates and invaders. Now it is scarcely visited. On leaving Roman Minturnae, I come at once upon the Garigliano River, and stop here to think of Spike Milligan. Here the soldier who became a comedian was traumatised by shell-shock.

I have no great expectations of today's long walk, but I feel I'm turning the corner and moving into the last stage of my journey. At last through the afternoon heat-haze I see the outline of Sessa Aurunca on a hill, and what I see makes me know it will be worth the detour. But first I must find the Ponte degli Aurunci, so I cross into a field where locals (I presume) are supervising a group of immigrant workers. No, they don't know a bridge of that name, but there is a big ruined bridge called "Ponte Ronaco". "That will do", I say. And it does.

Soon I'm looking up at it. Yes, this is the bridge which carried the old *Appia* over the marshes, hence its many arches, a viaduct rather than a bridge. It needs attention, but may it be spared restoration. I like its untidiness. I do not intend to ask about any local legends because I fear that this hump-backed bridge will be associated with some story of St. Martin and the devil, and I prefer it without either.

Up to Sessa Aurunca, a town I had not seen until today. A dome is visible, covered in tiles of green and jellow majolica, a foretaste of the south. There are rounded towers and a gate, through which I enter and walk through the narrow streets. The Duomo is a gem: not too pristine, nor clinically restored. A tiny porch with roof tiles and arches was built all those centuries ago against my coming, to shelter me from the sun. There are story-book carvings growing out of the pagan stone.

The church is dedicated to St. Peter. Did he oust Mercury the god of trade? I go on a treasure-hunt in this tiny space. Episodes from the *Acts of the Apostles* are everywhere. Fully captioned carvings leave no doubt that this is Simon the Magician. And here is the life of Peter. Were not Peter and Paul both travellers on this road? Well then, here they are pictured in a brotherly embrace.

How crucial was this New Testament book for the early Christian community? It was the latest news off the press. But it is little read now! I go into the church. I will forgive them for all the stucco and flim-flam. A marble carpet leads me to a high Cosmatesque pulpit, whose corner carvings could have graced a provincial temple.

It is signed by one Pellegrino. A travelling sculptor? As I look at a waterfont carved from an old pagan capital, a local sitting in a corner has noticed my interest and soon he is helping me to discover more. For a long time we stand by the pulpit. I mention Jonah, and he leads me to carvings I would certainly have missed. First the sea monster, genuinely beautiful, squamous and most un-whale like. He does not call it a 'Balena' (a whale) but a 'pistrice' (a shark), and it does look more like the latter.

The prophet is magnificent as he thunders at the Ninivites who sit with their king outside the city wall. But Jonah is due to be disappointed, the people are contrite and will surely be spared by God. Hereabouts along the route Jonah is everywhere as if by popular demand. Did the weary traveller by now start asking himself, "What am I doing here?" and " Is my journey really necessary?" Jonah thought that way.

After thanks and greetings, my guide takes his leave and I go down into the columned crypt, and allow myself to be refreshed. I'm even tempted to keep going right for Bari, but I'll keep to my plan of taking a break at Capua, one day's walk ahead.

Friday 25th July I look down at the five stones I left yesterday in the Duomo Porch. It is early morning and I am resigned to the fact that I shall not be able to look again into this little treasure chest. I look up through the railings at Peter and Paul flanking the enthroned Christ. Dare I call myself a fellow traveller?

I walk out of the gate and down to the road which leads to Capua, my last stage for the present. On another day, or if I were in better health, I'd be tempted to make side trips. I can see a distant castle. Is Carinola as lovely as its name?

Sparanise will do for a midday halt. I have cheese and water, but no bread; I am just in time, I think, to go into the local bakery. The good shopkeeper is genuinely mortified. He has sold his last small loaf. But then he remembers and bids me wait, while he goes through to his own domestic kitchen and comes back with a large round loaf and a knife, cuts the loaf in half, shares it and prints me a bill for ten cents.

Good things happen. He has a pilgrim's blessing. Fortified by this food I make for Capua. The traffic is increasing and I can see a great highway ahead, even as I cross a railway line. Capua was always crucial on the road map.

It was here that the first *Via Appia* ended, till it was extended to Benevento and alternative routes to the sea ports were opened up.

There are two towns, or rather Capua has shifted between two sites.

I come to the curved Volturno river and cross the Ponte Romano under the beady eye of a ruined tower. Since it is familiar territory I shall not linger, though I do salute the severed heads rescued from a temple in old Capua and now set in the wall of a municipal building on the main square.

But I will take time to visit the Museo Campano in a former convent, now a shrine to the "Matres Matutae" (that is, pagan symbols of fertility). These are pre-Roman pottery statues of wide motherly figures enthroned and holding two or three babies each. Such images were banned by the Church; no pilgrim will have seen them but something of their spirit lives on in statues of the Madonna and Child.

I'm not doing Capua justice, but I have to reach Santa Maria in Capua Vetere, 132 miles from Rome. In imperial times it is claimed a messenger using relays of fast horses might get here in two days and I have taken ten on the road. Of the two towns of Capua this has the more ancient roots, and has claims on Hannibal, Spartacus and every invading barbarian. I seek out the amphitheatre, massive even in its ruined state, though I realise that the great rebel slave would not recognise a single stone of it, only the site. I walk the pleasant but very provincial streets and wonder how Hannibal was supposed to have been so softened by the sybaritic luxury of the town that he had no fight left in him and succumbed to the Romans. I find the Mithraeum and its custodian, and sit in the frescoed cave, and think of the middle-class, male, military cult which was swamped by Christianity.

But all the time I have half an eye open for Abbot Nikulaus, and I am not disappointed. He has made it here by the high road and speaks specially of Cassino of Benedictine fame.

He takes no interest at all in my stories of ghosts of the pagan past but speaks with enthusiasm of the Medical School of Salerno. As we look south over the plain, he swings his arm vaguely towards Neapolis, the new city, and speaks of new discoveries in medicine as other medievals might speak of the latest miracle worker. While I have been looking to a dead past, his thoughts are all on the future.

I cannot restrain him. I have not the energy to pursue him.

I go back to the once triple-arch of Hadrian, the sad philosopher who found solace here rather than in his costly villa near Tivoli and I salute his vague wandering soul which cannot even give me its customary wistful smile.

Whilst Abbot Nikulaus seeks out Naples I shall also go south to Calabria to stay in a monastery with a lay religious community.

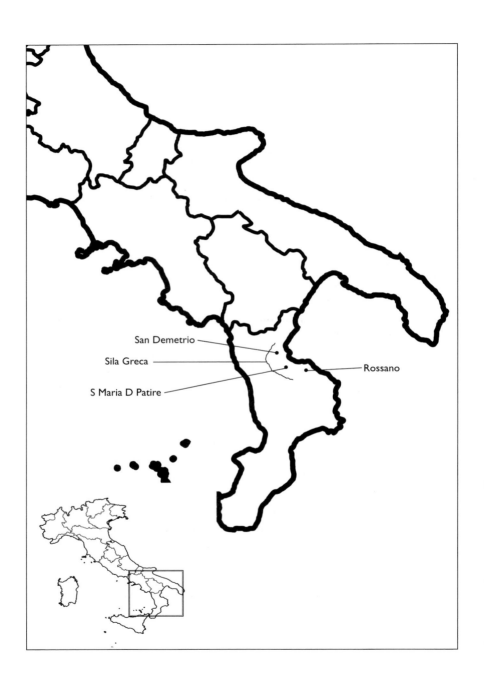

San Demetrio

Sila Greca

S Maria D Patire

Rossano

158

INTERLUDE
BY THE IONIAN SEA

I took sanctuary in Santa Maria delle Grazie beneath the hill-top of Rossano in Calabria, which overlooks the Ionian Sea. Nothing but water separated us from Greece or from Africa.

The lay community welcomed me, as they had done half a dozen times in the past. Their day is ordered, and centered on prayer, they are linked with justice and peace and third-world projects. They also welcome youth groups from as far away as Puglia and the Molise. After a total rest here, I wished to go to Greek Patirion, and then visit Rossano. The ancient Albanian towns would not refuse us, I'm sure. So a group of us set out.

There are roads now to the ancient monasteries, and the Patirion is well signposted, but we chose to scramble through the woods, where goats and deer at first looked up at us in surprise and continued grazing. We crossed streams on tree trunks thoughtfully felled for us by those who made the route, but we knew that in the springtime we and everything in the narrow gorge would have been swept along by the "torrente".

Norman Douglas was here in the early twentieth century and spoke of pebbly stream-beds and an odorous tangle of cistus, rosemary and myrtle, of a forest of enormous chestnuts, oaks, hollies and Calabrian pines emerging out of an ocean of glittering bracken. Nothing has changed.

But the famous monastery, the Patirion mostly a ruin now, drew us on. Today, both male and female visitors may enter the church promiscuously without let or hindrance, and view the images or simply enjoy its peace. What has always attracted me is the floor with its mosaics, naïve, lively and full of animals and mythology. But these were never designed for the profane eyes of tourists, and the Basilian monks were refugees not from political enemies but from the world itself.

Douglas, who is mostly sympathetic to the cultures he encounters, and is tolerant even of superstition, excoriates the thousands of hermits who populated the area in the middle ages. I have visited some of their dwellings, and it is quite true they do not have en-suite bathrooms. No Victorian bigot could better his account of the damage that these bestial aboriginals did to humanity. And, if we are to believe him, monastic communities only came into being because the supply of bat-infested caves had dried up. These too, it would seem were vile in every respect, but attracted vast multitudes to an unclean life of matted hair and superstition. Marvellous stuff. Keep it up Norman. There were at least 200 monasteries in Calabria, now in varying stages of ruin. A few survive as living communities.

The youth group who were with us reacted as positively to prayer and meditation in the monastery as they did to rambling through the savage woods.

Rossano is not Italian, any more than any village around here is Italian. Each venerable place has its own tale, which is not a continuous story. Like sand-castles, they survive the high tide, to flourish for a time and await the next onslaught. They have served as a refuge for ancient Greeks fleeing civil strife and creating here a string of colonies which became Magna Graecia, admired envied and occasionally sacked by the Romans. The Byzantines too, a very different breed but speaking the same language, set up church and shop to recolonise the barbarian west. Over the centuries they have been at the mercy of foreign overlords, and northern Italian landowners. But the greatest plague of all has been economic necessity which has caused a mass exodus in almost every generation. So much so that many towns depend on the 'Americani', locals who have prospered abroad, and either send money back home or return to spend their gains locally. That is no kind of economy. But anything rooted locally struggles to survive.

Even the ancient Albanian culture, should it be forced to perform for tourists, as Inuits and reservation Indians are made to perform in the USA, will, I fear, lose its soul. All along the coast there is a rootless tourist trade, exchanging money for sun-tan. There is, however, no problem with drunkenness: the English do not get this far.

With the help of friends I sought out the Albanian townships, San Demetrio Città and Spezzano Albanese. There the descendants of those who fled the Turks in the fifteenth century, found refuge and took root. They cling to the hills, to their language and to their customs. Their liturgies are in ancient Albanian, Greek and Italian in equal measure, and since they are at one with Rome I am able to participate and celebrate with them, but a villager steps in to read the parts which are in fifteenth-century Albanian.

When in Calabria, I carry as a constant companion and talisman, a *Dictionarium Latino-Epiroticum* (Latin–Medieval Albanian) of 1635, which provides amusement and enlivens conversation in the cafe after Mass. These people despise modern Albanian and speak a very ancient version.

I love their nostalgic, sad, self-indulgent stories of the magic, mythical, heroic past, when they speak of their sainted hero-martyr Skanderberg or more correctly Georgio Castriotis, who, in Albania, vainly struggled against the invading, rampant Turk. The Albanians fled and landed here. For more than three centuries intrepid travellers were fascinated by these gentle reserved, inward-looking people. There are still over 80,000 of them scattered among the Albanese towns of Calabria and Sicily.

Modern roads and communications will, I fear, make it difficult for these people to remain in suspended animation.

From the Sanctuary the road to Rossano is steep. Two thirds of the way up, I stopped on a curve, sat down and looked back, and drew out notes I had copied from *Old Calabria* by Norman Douglas, the English exile: "Down a many-folded gorge of glowing red earth decked with olives and cistus the eye wanders to the Ionian sea shining in deepest turquoise tints and beautified by a glittering margin of white sand".

In Rossano, Douglas sought the famed *Codex Purpureus*, a late fifth-century Byzantine Gospel, written on parchment in gold and silver letters, the capitals decorated in the costliest colours available, and with full page illustrations of the gospel scenes,. The local town secretary, who was less than gracious, passed him on to the delightful and erudite Canonico Rizzo who was familiar with English literature, including Milton and the Puritans, and knew recent English history too, as well as that of Byzantium. And the Codex? Yes, he would show it to the visitor, but he did not consider himself an authority on it.

On this visit I had no difficulties. The Tourist Office directed me to the Cathedral Museum. I rang the doorbell and, since the hour was reasonable, I was given the freedom of the rooms which once were part of the Bishop's Palace, now housing a collection of ornaments, documents and reliquaries, and here the Codex has pride of place. I wished to kneel before this venerable text, but instead I stood silently as before a living presence. This is the only Greek New Testament manuscript containing pictures of the life of Christ and dating from the dangerous days of Iconoclasm. A rare, precious, marvellous survival. On this my sixth visit I saw my sixth page. They turn the pages slowly.

Out into the street, and in by the side door of the cathedral. It is Byzantine with Gothic overlay and its jewel is the picture of the Madonna, one of many Acheiropita. Sometimes it seems that there are only two classes of paintings of Mary from the early period:

those painted by St. Luke (when he was not practising medicine) and those painted by angels.

Downhill I went past the five-domed church of San Marco, clinically restored, but still beautiful, almost like a black and white photograph of the more famous Cattolica at Stilo, and I looked back at Rossano, which, *pace* the guidebooks, is not named for the reddish colour of its crumbling cliffs. Procopius tells us it is named after the landowner Roscianus. As the town increases in age it diminishes in size, and the steep surrounding gullies fill up with the debris of falling houses.

I went back to the Sanctuary in the plain and to my community of Santa Maria. The monastery has a garden, and within its narrow compass are trees bearing every local fruit. They keep bees which have no need to forage beyond the garden walls. I have never met more pacific bees. In the evening whoever is a guest is invited to sit with the community at long tables to share simple fare and to drink the uncomplicated local wine. I sat and listened to the music of the voices and reflected that in all my journey so far I had met and talked with strangers, far too briefly, and at no depth. I had been made welcome in religious communities, who had no obligation to me except their own need to fulfill the Gospel. I had by arrangement met up with friends, always to my benefit. But here, specially here, there is no difference between stranger and friend. It is something very Greek. Their language has only one word for stranger and quest. Each house, each community, is a 'zenodochium', a place which welcomes strangers.

Not only had my health improved, I felt more at ease with my little project of walking the length of Italy.

Having stepped back I could see that it was like walking across a table-top map. There is a community in Rome which leaves a large jig-saw on a table in the common room. Any member or quest, may add a piece at will. On this journey I've been putting down the pieces carefully and in set order. I shall soon be going back to the table to add a piece or two. I am aware that I have one great advantage over medieval pilgrims: I have maps, and so I do not have to rely on hearsay. Looking back on my route I can see that the *Via Francigena* follows a fairly straight line, give or take a mountain or two, from Switzerland to the Campania. Over the centuries almost by common agreement and allowing for individual needs the shortest and safest route was established and written into folklore

On this journey I have revisited many places which I have known these forty years or more. But still I'm not sure that I have the whole picture, because Italy has four dimensions, the last being the unexpected. Nearly everyone I have met would call themselves Italian, but, though they all have many characteristics in common, belonging to one nation is not one of them. Italy has never been one. It has, willy-nilly, received many new civilisations and new cultures, but the experience of each region and the way it has absorbed other cultures is unique to that region. The survival-alliances forced upon regions and cities from prehistoric times often set one region or city against its neighbours.

San Giovanni Rotondo
Ceringola
Canosa
Andria
Bari
Monopoli
Capua
Benevento
Brindisi
Lecce
Otranto
Santa Maria

166

Capua to Santa Maria:
2nd August-25th September

Appius Claudius the Censor, blind benefactor of humanity, designed the road which eventually reached Italy's furthest parts.

The *Appia* linked Rome with the gateway ports to the Levant. It allowed two-way traffic for the postal services and helped to create the empire. After the fall of Rome, with the conflict of private interests, whole sections of the road reverted to mule tracks, but merchants and armies still used it for want of anything better.

Returning to Capua Vetere, I take stock once more. I'm looking forward to teaming up with medieval monks again, and with pilgrims who, for safety, attached themselves to the caravans and armies moving south. They were ever grateful for the help and protection of those much maligned enthusiasts the Templars and Hospitallers.

It was in Capua Vetere that Abbot Nikolaus and I parted as we went our different ways south; he to learn of the scientific advances of the eleventh-century medicine in Salerno, I to take a cure and take stock in a monastery in Calabria. Here I also read up the Itinerary of Bernard the Frenchman and two other monks (one of them Stephen the Spaniard). The ninth-century memorial records how they reached Rome and spoke with the pope. It was good of the Pontiff to see them, as he was embroiled in political negotiations with the Carolingian party, trying to keep the independence of the

Papal See, and then there was that never-ending theological wrangle (the "Filioque" dispute) with the Greeks. Personally, I think that if you asked the average Christian (Latin or Greek) "Does the Spirit come from the Father alone, or from the Father through the Son, or from both directly?" they might be tempted to change the subject sharpish. God laughs at our maths.

But these three monks "brothers in devotion and charity", shared their plans with the pope, saying how they would aim for Beneventum and then Monte Gargano on the spur of the boot of Italy, and if they could find no ship there, they would make straight down the coast for Bari, though it was at that time a 'Saracen city'. Bright-eyed and fresh from blessing, they will have passed by Capua Vetere, but it was probably ruinous from numerous Saracen raids. A new town was being built to replace it on the curve of the River Volturno. As monks however they would have plenty of options at the Benedictine foundations which were springing up all around, spreading out from Cassino.

Tomorrow, I'll make a new start, but I realise that my plan is slightly changed.

I remember a couple of years ago hearing a government spokesman on education comparing people who were "goal-orientated" with those who were "experience-orientated", the modern equivalent I suppose, of Platonists and Aristotelians. The trouble is, he was right. The nearer I get to my goal the more I want to concentrate on the experience. Something else has changed.

All my journey so far has been centred on Rome. Even though I have left it 150 miles behind, I have, metaphorically been looking backwards, looking over my shoulder to that city. Now there is no looking back, I've worked out a valid route to the Adriatic, each section of which was used by pilgrims, and I shall walk every mile of it, but I have the time and inclination to stray from it in the company of pilgrims who made other choices, and then to return to my chosen path. Thus with the help of St. Nicholas I shall accomplish my vow.

Sunday 3rd August. The stroll from Capua Vetere to Caserta holds no romance.

Modern constructions on one side, a long prison wall on the other. Ahead is the famous Reggia, most grandiose of all Italian palaces. I cannot like it. I am trying not to hate it. It seems that in all its 250 years it has always been either a-building or in restoration.

In 1752 at the ceremony of laying the first stone they deployed an army to trace its outline as on a map. Nowadays it is outlined by corrugated iron sheets and orange plastic net curtains. I am told that the present gargantuan complex is a reduced version of Vanvitelli's original design.

Leaflets offer statistics about its great length and vast number of rooms. The decorated halls were the scene of many a lavish hunting party and masked ball. Spanish tyrants and King Bomba the Bad of Naples held court here The singularly unvictorious King Victor Emmanuel III bestowed this palace on a grateful nation and the German forces surrendered here to Field Marshal Alexander.

If medieval pilgrims had known what they were missing, they would doubtless have been grateful. I shall hurry by and go up the hill to Caserta Vecchia, where what remains of a dignified old town is preserved and even lived in, mainly by artists and comfortable people who wish to live away from the bustle of the modern city below. In its heyday (the twelfth and thirteenth centuries) it benefited from Appian trade and from Norman military might. I rest my back against the solid campanile of the cathedral, which wisely in this earthquake zone is free standing. Inside the church I discover that the Normans, though they were skilled artists and builders, were not above borrowing columns from the pagans to line the nave. They added Christian carvings to adorn the pulpit. Once outside again I climb to a vantage point. Here the air is lighter on the lungs. The village crowns a hill which drops steeply into a ravine. I have to accept that if the local villages are still standing it is probably thanks to the castle nearby which keeps a wary eye on southern Campania. I tip my pilgrim's hat to the military.

Once back in Caserta I'm staying near the railway station in a hotel which is in a slightly higher league than my usual *pensione*, and in the evening I go next door to a restaurant. Good food is set before me but I have scarcely tucked in my napkin when a moustachioed middle-aged commercial traveller sits back to back with my chair and over his shoulder he sends clouds of tobacco smoke. So I get up and go to the desk at the door in protest, before walking out, making it obvious that I don't intend to pay. Will the manager be sympathetic? Will he call me back? Will he command the miscreant to stop smoking? No. He shrugs his shoulders, and does not even remove the cigarette from his own lips as he vaguely waves goodbye.

Wednesday 6ᵗʰ August. It is about ten miles from Caserta to Santa Maria. I'll go there and still have time to hitch-hike up into the hills to Saint Agatha of the Goths. It is still early. I am on the road but not fully awake when a young couple sitting in a car where a side road meets the *Appia* call me over, and say they are American. He is Brazilian, I'd guess, and she hardly speaks, but I'm sure she is Italian. "Can you explain this money", he says, showing me some Lira notes. I say, "They use the Euro now". So he asks me to show him the new notes and I lean on the open window and open my wallet. "Does each note have a number?", he says, his nose practically touching a fifty Euro note. "Can I look closer? Are there any hotels near here?" I wake up and extract myself. I wave them towards Caserta and continue south. How could I have been so stupid and trusting, and why didn't they rob me? For the rest of the day I feel uneasy and annoyed with myself.

Meanwhile, I pass a barracks. I should think there has probably been a military presence here without interruption since the time of the Roman Republic. The only thing that has changed is the name of the soldiers' paymasters.

Santa Maria a Vico is small, and strings itself along the *Appia* like a decade of the rosary. It is proud to have an old Chapel of the Congregation of Loreto. Somehow devotion to the mobile House of Nazareth has reached here from the Marche. Even more important is the connection with St. Alphonsus Ligouri, an eighteenth-century Neapolitan lawyer full of the milk of human kindness. He gave up the legal profession in disgust when he was tripped up in court by the complexity of the laws in Campania, which derive from so many contradictory cultures and traditions. The Law Courts' loss was the Church's gain. He wrote books on morality which today would be considered legalistic, but they are relatively compassionate. Today his devotional books are having a new vogue. When he was made Bishop of Sant' Agata dei Goti, just to the north, he walked humbly and sought justice for the poor people, and they've not forgotten it. Here in Santa Maria they put up a marble inscription to him next to the parish church which he restored in dreadful style. I get a bus up to his episcopal city, St. Agatha of the Goths, not just to honour the good bishop of this area but also because I'm convinced that most pilgrims who got this far will at least have over-nighted there. The old town is built as on a cliff, hanging over a torrent, and the houses seem to spring from the living rock.

The specific title 'of the Goths' is quite recent, but it is good that at last the dear old Goths get a mention. They weren't here long, and they were ousted by the Byzantines, who in their turn suffered at the hands of the Lombards, who were overwhelmed by the Normans, who …

Here I'm looking for an old friend, Christopher, and I meet him again, once in the Duomo, and once in the Annunziata. St Christopher has every right to be here, as the Isclero torrent is difficult and dangerous to cross. His services were needed by pilgrims. There is a beautiful renaissance lunette of the Annunciation and Gabriel on the left bids me enter and accept the salvation which is announced. But I am drawn up short by the Doom on the door, a fresco of the fifteenth century.

Scenes of Hell and damnation were popular from before the

171

time of Dante right through to Milton, and here fornicators and traitors get the treatment. The strangest figure of all is Julian the Apostate who is being tortured by bat-winged, cow-horned demons. With naïve faith in recorded history, I had thought that Julian was a fourth-century pagan emperor who reversed the policy of tolerating Christians, and I could understand why he should be consigned to Hell. But the artist story-teller has put him there for a different reason. Apparently Julian was a renegade pope, and there he is, wearing a fourteenth-century papal tiara (and nothing else) to prove it. I recall that in Dante's time Mahomet was placed by some in the part of Hell reserved for renegade Christians.

Pilgrims must have been tempted to stay on in Sant'Agata. The Cathedral crypt is a delight with re-used columns topped by crude but striking capitals. The monks of St. Menna, near the only bridge, provided shelter in their church which is a miniature version of the basilica, with rounded apse, small rounded windows, Cosmatesque floor, marbled and gated enclosure which separated the people from the clergy physically, but not from sharing in sight and sound, since the people could gather all around.

These stopping places saw so much traffic passing below them that pilgrims will have had to take their chance alongside merchants and soldiers. Northern Campania has always been at the mercy of the next invader.

By this time the bulk of the pilgrims is no longer with us. The stream of pilgrims divides as in a delta. Of those who have come beyond Rome, many are now seeking any port on the Tyrrhenian sea which will offer them safe passage to the east. They will work their way round the southern coast until they find a boat.

Santa Maria a Vico to Benevento
There was a time when every schoolchild was taught about the brave Samnites who defeated the Romans at the meeting of the ways, (Furculae Caudinae) the Caudine Forks.

I had hoped this pass on which I was entering would live up to the story, but in the first light of dawn the view towards Benevento presented no terrors.

Local information leaflets stress, with not a little poetic licence that "we are all Samnites here", and it is possible that the odd Samnite blood cell may still be floating around among the local peasantry.

This warlike tribe, cousins of Rome's first enemies the Sabines had one resounding victory over the Republican armies in 321BC. The Romans had first tried to isolate the Samnites from their allies (divide and rule) but were themselves holed up in this wide but bottle-necked valley, and they were attacked from every side. When two Consular armies were sent to force the issue they too were trapped in the valley, starved into surrender and forced to pass beneath a yoke of spears.

Later the Romans, when sated with bloody success, could afford the luxury of relishing their greatest defeats (Cannae, Trasimene and the Caudine Forks) much as the British speak of Gallipoli and Dunkirk, and the Anglo Saxons remember that their forefathers were overwhelmed by the Normans.

I'm looking down on the sight of a massacre, but this is no Glencoe. This is a happy smiling Campania Felix, though by midday at 37 °C the smile is wearing thin. Ahead lies a very straight Roman road, and Montesarchio, the last fortified village before Beneventum.

Horace stayed near here with friends. He rarely needed a hotel. They had a banquet of roasted thrushes, but the barbecue nearly burned the house down. Is that smoke I can see rising across the valley though the heat haze?

At Montesarchio I sit in the triangle of the crossroads (it is a real Trivium). I eat bread and cheese and drink a glass of local wine, and look up at the Bourbon fortress where patriots were held for having rebelled against the latest foreign tyrants.

Beneventum is by name 'the town of good omen'. The Romans claimed that before they arrived it used to be called 'Maleventum'.

Today it gets a bad press in the guide books. Its centre was devastated in the last war and like London it was badly rebuilt. But I was well treated here and met only with good luck.

It may be that the River Sabato, running through the town, an ancient haunt of witches (hence the name witches sabbath) makes it of evil omen. Most Italians believe in witches and fear them. Ask them about it.

The town trades on the name Strega (witches' brew) and claims the drink as its own. Benevento is full of magical surprises, even the bombing reveals its ancient roots and a Roman theatre. A solid soulless alley may lead to trimmed ruins, a bland restored facade may take us into a vibrant church. Along the same main street which leads to the Castle the bombs have spared a Byzantine round church and a Lombard cloister, and near to them the most beautiful Roman Triumphal Arch in all the Empire.

Trajan was (rightly) venerated here as a saint. Blessed are the road makers. In A.D. 108-110 he dragged the line of the Appia northwards, and by means of viaducts he cut a swathe to Brindisi. So the Beneventans in 114 A.D. were not surprised to see him described as 'optimus' in this arch which was the gateway to the East and to prosperity. It is a fine work of propoganda. On it he is depicted being ever so kind to the deserving poor, and the inscription speaks of 'Felicitas Temporum' 'we've never had it so good' they told themselves, as they hastened to get the momument ready for his return from his eastern campaigns.

In the evening I go to S. Sophia. The cloister is open and I can look closely at the capitals on the columns. Here we have both Hercules as a hero and all the biblical figures wrestling with evil.

Pilgrims were indebted to Trajan for this road, and they also needed the protection of whoever was most powerful at the moment - so I go into the round church to dedicate my evening prayer to those who made pilgrimage possible.

Writers have described this church as gloomy, but I find it peaceful as I let the psalms sink in. After a while I realise that a priest has been sitting nearby, and so we go to the sacristy and I begin to talk shop with Don Nazzareno Tenga.

I share something of my pilgrimage, and he very openly, and in a pastoral manner, speaks of the worries of running the diocese of which he is Vicar General. As I listen I appreciate how fortunate I am to be on Sabbatical.

Going east from Benevento there never has been one route. Many favoured the Gargano to the north west. Here St. Michael was the great draw, as was the port of Siponto, and, if no boat was to be found there, pilgrims could scour the eastern shore of Puglia from Barletta down to Otranto.

I shall steer a middle way to Bari, visit the ports and then go south down the coast, but at all times I shall welcome the temptation to take side trips.

It is well known that Horace took this route when he was bound for Greece, but he travelled before Trajan had worked his miracles of engineering, whereas the pilgrims travelled after the emperor's wonderway had crumbled to dust. Horace was well-connected, and could rely on friends for hospitality. Indeed, his own villa, a perk from the emperor, lay on the more southerly road to Taranto under Monte Vulture, which dominates everything south of the *Appia*. Pilgrims were less favoured and had to rely on hostelries. They were the brave ones. From this point, pilgrims would begin to hear rumours that Jerusalem was closed once more, or that Bari was in Saracen hands. Some were discouraged and made do with a substitute Holy Sepulchre, or some minor goal, and went home.

There were many who were deeply grateful to the Templars for safe lodging, and agreed to be escorted by them, or by the armies of the Lombards or Byzantines, asking to be led to the next place of safety. In the earliest days of pilgrimage, in the fourth century, the valiant Lady Egeria accepted a Roman military escort in Arabia "for as long as we travelled through suspicious places". One reason why I cannot find evidence of a chain of hostels is that no route dominated. Another is that local people are very vague on the subject, and finally, Renato Stopani, the great authority, has not, as far as I know, completed his work on the southern section of the *Via Francígena*. I'm not rushing. First, I want to get a view of the Puglian plain, so I'll make a very short walk to Paduli.

We are gaining height, and must be near the watershed, with a commanding view to the east. But it does not materialise and I'll have to settle for exploring the River Calore, which lives up to its name (warmth). It is like a trickle from a hot water tap. Bleached boulders are too hot to walk on barefoot. No doubt there are times when it is a raging torrent, but now it is scarcely two feet deep. Of Paduli: I learn only one thing, that it has always been defenceless. Its greatest claim to fame is that it has been ravaged by more savages than any other comparable town. First by Pyrrhus, then by Carthage, then by Goths and Visigoths, Ostrogoths, Lombards, Spaniards, Normans, Swabians and Aragonese. Is there anyone who has not ravaged Paduli? I have better hopes of Buonalbergo. With a name like that, surely it will provide an answer to my question about accommodation for pilgrims.

Tuesday 12th August. I need time to look for Roman bridges, relics of that masterly Trajanic achievement: the road which leapt from hill to hill and brooked no obstacle. Here the local people help me, and so I am able to string together a line of at least three bridges. First, the Ponte Valentino. It endured to medieval times, and acquired a saint's name. It also has a beautiful Gothic shape to it. I know that Forum Novum was somewhere near here, but can find no clue. I've firmly decided to give locals a chance to inform or misinform me. That's how pilgrims fared, and so someone takes me by the hand to the Ponte dei Ladroni. I take it that the bridge was notorious for ambushes. What remains of it is unimpressive, but it is good to splash along the shallow river. My companion thinks I'm "matto" (crazy, a term they often apply to the English) but he joins in, and then leaves me with a kindly warning about vipers. Next, the Ponte delle Chianche, more like an ivy-clad viaduct. I'm on my own once more, and I cross the glistening, smooth, wet bed-rock where in spring there must be a little waterfall and rapids. All around is scrub and thorn-bushes. Through the heat haze I can see that there is a gentle slope to lead me up to Buonalbergo. Modern tarmac takes over from the Strada Bianca, and I arrive hot and tired in Buonalbergo, where ancient and modern lie side by side. At the cafe on the square by the church, they already know about the English traveller who asks a lot of questions and likes ruined bridges. I intend to order the largest bottle of water they have, but find myself led to a seat, and surrounded by people eager to answer any questions I can throw at them. I don't see any hotels, so I say "Are there some hotels hidden away?" I find out that in fact the name Buonalbergo doesn't really refer to a Hotel, but to the vast slope above the town where huge flocks of sheep rested during the annual migration (Transumanza) from the Abruzzi mountains into the plains. "And where is the ancient Forum Novum?" I ask. "Why, right here", say some, though others disagree. In this lively discussion I sense a genuine welcome. They even share with me some more recent history, telling me how the Church of San Donato had collapsed in 1895, minutes before the people were due to assemble. The cafe-owner who has provided us all with water and glasses, will not think of payment, and so, to a chorus of 'Auguri' worthy of a benign sitting of Roman seers fresh from inspecting birds' entrails, I leave. But first I go to the church. On the wall an inscription reads "For the greatness of the miracle, for the faith of his followers, this church rises in more splendid form, 1898". I go in to salute the statue and the saint. You can't argue with facts. Then I go steeply down, passing more Roman ruins, and I remember that they mentioned a little church "Madonna della Macchia" and find a seventeenth-century chapel (for once I think it is not a medieval church which has been "improved"). The story is that it was built to house a wooden Madonna and Child found in the woods (Macchia). I wonder was this the accepted euphemism for catching it as it fell off the back of a lorry? Now I set down five small stones on the S.90 and return to Benevento where I have made provision for one more night.

Many pilgrims arriving at Buonalbergo will have asked directions for Troia. The hills to the north look daunting. For the moment I shall keep to the S.90 because it will take me to places mentioned in the old itineraries. But I shall soon make a break to the north to visit Troia, Lucera and the Gargano, because the season of feasts and processions is upon us, and I'd like to be there to celebrate.

This is only a token stretch to make it easier later, then I shall resume serious walking. First, a nod in the direction of Ponte Santa Maria. The pilgrim Mother of Christ crossed many a bridge in her time. For the first time I have cramp in the leg muscles. Is it the extremely dry weather?

No matter: from tomorrow I'll be hitching lifts or using public transport for three or four days. I intend to explore a little, leave the pilgrimage route I had set down, and go north before resuming my walk. The reason is as follows.

This area of Italy was spoken of as a delta; the pilgrims could reach the ports as far north as Siponto in the Gargano or as far south as Bari in Apulia and the whole region was criss-crossed by pilgrim tracks. I wish to take in several of the most famous stopping-places, and as this is the high season for feasts I can attend three of them and visit two shrines of international renown. Troia of the disreputable name (do not address a lady by the title) is a town with a proud history. I get there by bus, knowing that others did a weary trek to get there. Now at last I can look across the 'Tavoliere', (table-top) and the view is like that from a balcony. Troia has a jewel-box of a cathedral. I don't know whether pilgrims consciously reacted to architecture or sculpture, comparing Byzantine, Pisan and Romanesque, noting Saracen influence, or whether they were simply overawed by the blend of beauty, the rose-window like lace, the bronze doors with their carvings. It is well know locally that one church-building Bishop of Troia had the surname Francigena. To recall the fact gives me the same feeling as I had in the early

1980s when, as a newcomer to London I found out that the Holloway Road was the A1: "Start walking from Highbury Corner I thought, and soon enough I would be in Gosforth Newcastle, where I lived for many years and, not long after that I would get to Alnwick where I was born. Here, in Italy, we are on the route of pilgrims or Frankish Merchants. The road itself was a boundary marker and reference point. May all notaries and those who settle boundary disputes be blest for recording boring details and may all conservators of dry documents receive their due reward. In a brief walk through the old quarter of Troia, I find the Hospital of St. John of God, and a record that the Fatebene Fratelli did good here. The medieval church now houses Evangelical Christians. (Should Christians be anything else?) I should not rush on, but I excuse myself because this is far from my first time here, and I've never seen Lucera which is celebrating a feast. Take it for granted that hereabouts any well-sited important little town will have been a tribal centre and then a Roman colony and will have an imposing castle usually provided by Frederick II in the thirteenth century. But Lucera is special, because the emperor, always at odds with the pope, brought 20,000 Saracens from Sicily and for fifty years, Lucera was a Muslim enclave, enjoying freedom of religion. Then came Charles of Anjou, who tried to convert them forcibly, and, having failed, went on to massacre them. I've been invited to take part in a solemn evening Mass to celebrate the seventh centenary of the cathedral. It was built on the ruins of the central Mosque, and I have some qualms because a large notice speaks of "the Infidels crushed down by the armies of Pipirio da Barletta, on the eve of the Assumption". The local clergy are most welcoming. The service is long, but mercifully free from triumphalism. The interim Bishop Francesco is interested in my journey, and speaks of his mother who, many years ago walked barefoot from Lucera to Monte San' Angelo, a distance of more than 60 miles

Do not expect much of Foggia, except good road and rail connections and a choice of hotels. The town was wiped out during the second world war, though the cathedral and a few of the old palaces survived. I'm here because I've heard that the procession for the Assumption runs under a different name. I cannot get the full story of the Madonna of the Seven Veils. It is quite decorous and concerns a statue found by peasants in a local bog. The veils stand for mystery. In Italy they have a habit of putting an individual stamp on universal feasts. The procession goes right through the modern city, making no concessions. Evening strollers and the café society react (or do not react) to the age-old rite. Now, here's a bonus. Today I've tracked down the church of St. Roch, beloved of pilgrims and by now a personal friend. Tomorrow is his feast. I'll be there.

Saturday 16ᵗʰ August. The little seventeenth-century church, full to the doors, is decked out and lit up. The priest speaks well of this northerner from an age of deadly plagues, whose fame has, with justification, travelled down the line. "Roch", he says, "had time to care for others as he journeyed. He risked his life for plague victims [I do wish the women would stop chattering]. He understood that life is a pilgrimage". When I first met St. Roch over 700 miles away at S. Rémy he was pointing at a boil on his right leg. Here he favours the left. After the services, I join the queue to kiss his relic.

I'm in the Gargano and I'm well aware that I'm setting off into an area which was already sacred when the gods were still young. There are buses, but every time I've been here I've hitch-hiked. On the outskirts of Foggia a tall, diffident German, seeking Padre Pio, gets out of his car to ask the way and he offers me a lift. I thank him, and suggest that we go by the coast road and see Siponto. He's surprised, as most modern pilgrims would be, to hear that anything else ever happened here in the whole of prehistory and history and that Gargano Promontory has anything else to offer but Padre Pio. But San Leonardo and Santa Maria di Siponto are two of the most moving churches in Italy, because of their setting, the ruins scattered around, the carvings and the columns. At San Leonardo besides the cathedral, there was a large building for storage (or for people?). What attracts is the whole bestiary of mythical and biblical animals. Santa Maria di Siponto was one of the chief ports of Italy, but of this nothing remains, since it was replaced by Manfredonia with its castle. They've uncovered Roman ruins at Santa Maria, but these are young compared with the cave-dwellings of Monte Sant' Angelo, in the hills inland from here, which were inhabited several thousand years before the Romans came.

We turn slightly back on ourselves to get to San Giovanni Rotondo, which is comfortably among the top ten places of pilgrimage in the world (if you omit Gracelands and Alton Towers). We find a place to park and make for the church where the Capuchin Stigmatist ministered. Then I use up all my German thanking this kind man for the lift, and we part. Each time I come to San Giovanni there are changes. I can remember when they expanded the little parish church to make a mausoleum for the holy man. He is there now, crystalised, and the people prayerfully circle in his underground tomb. The friars and volunteers set themselves the task of pastoral ministry here and in the adjoining friary. But now I go back into the blazing sun and down the wide steps. How the town has grown! The hospital dominates the hillside. There is an open-air Way of the Cross carved into the living rock. A vast new church will soon accommodate multiples of thousands.

There are day-pilgrims, and for the others there is accommodation ranging from the luxurious to the plain and simple. They are all attracted by a friar who never left Campania and the Abruzzi, at least not in the flesh. Lives have been changed for the good. Traditionally, and for very good reasons, the Church gives a hard time to those who attract a following during their lifetime, and all canonisations are posthumous.

Pilgrim spots are often very remote. This wild mountain, seemingly at the end of the world, has attracted first pagans and then Christians, to worship in their own way, as so often happens. I now take a local bus, and the mountain road to a pilgrim site

Monte Sant' Angelo which is at least 1,400 years older than San Giovanni.

The first apparition of St. Michael Archangel and Warrior is placed in Lombard times somewhere in the fifth century, but for 1000 years it had already been a sacred site Most people know that the Lombards were powerful once in northern Italy (hence Lombardy) but they also had a kingdom in the south and spent centuries defending it against Normans and Byzantines, with the help of St. Michael. When the Lombards were defeated Northmen and Greeks claimed Michael for their own.

I make my own way down under a beautiful arch and through bronze doors down a flight of stairs into a cave. So many pilgrims have come here! For centuries it was on a par with Rome. Here, it is pointed out, St. Francis, a great pilgrim, sat and prayed. I sit in relative peace. The thought darts: "What if this is also a pre-Christian sacred place?" The whole mountain is a Gruyère Cheese of prehistoric dwellings.

This Christian shrine has been restored; stucco and late improvements have been removed, and I can see rough carvings of hands and feet, which for millennia have been the signs left by those who sought a numinous presence, mainly up mountains and in caves. What is simplest in art is most difficult to date. There is also a renaissance statue, by Sansovino they say, which shows the Archangel as a bit of a softie, hardly able to lift his languid eyelids, never mind a sword. To choose St. Michael as your patron is to aim high. There are only two references to him in the Bible, *The Book of Daniel* and *Revelation*s (two books loved and selectively quoted by every crackpot fanatic). In *Daniel* chapter 10 Michael is "One of the leading Princes" and valiant against the Persians.

In *Revelations* 12, Michael whose name means "Who is like to God?", casts out the dragon and decisively settles the war between the angels. And this is why they made him the protector of imperialist armies. But down in the deepest cave is a simpler version of the saint in knee-length tunic, winged, and lightly stepping forward and looking after the world, a little globe in his right hand. I've been sitting a while here. The cave is mystic, atmospheric, moving. Pilgrimages were invented for places like this, and vice-versa.

Back to the surface. I pay a visit to the Tomba dei Rotari. Years ago, guide books translated that as a tomb, or burial place. In fact it is an eccentric baptistery with a gloriously high dome, a man-made cave with carvings. Tomorrow down to earth, and back to the road, and the continuation of my pilgrmage.

Monday 18th August Now that I've explored the more northerly pilgrim routes I'll return to my main journey. I'll set myself a target. Five days to Canosa. With daily temperatures in the mid-thirties, I need to go in short stages. Each day by 9 in the morning it is uncomfortably hot. On the road as I think of entering a pub, two large hounds come at me, fangs bared, and one even flings himself sideways at me clipping my elbow. Two men come out and are amused. Not I. "Control them", I shout, but the dogs slink away anyhow and I walk on. For a few miles I've been plagued by huge hardbacked horseflies which hover in a cloud around my head. One gets into my eye and fixes his pincers into my eyelid. He will not let go. I have to yank him off and part of me goes with him. Worse, half a dozen of his mates climb down the gap between my backpack and me, and, with jaws that pierce my shirt, feast on my shoulders. A plague on them, these late-arriving, 'Malae Culices', Horace warned me of in Terracina.

A mile further on I see a roadside cafe and sit down at a table in the shade, thirsty and tired, but no one comes out, so I make do with a short rest. At Bovino, there is a higher village, and a cluster of houses below, round a railway halt. I enter a gated complex. Tiredness gives me the energy to ignore the signs saying "This is a power station. The public must not enter". I find a bench under a tree. A worker approaches me, not to order me out off the premises, but to invite me into an office, where his companion sits at a wooden table. They pour out water for me, and ask me what I am doing. As they get interested, one of them slips out to tell a local family and soon several of us are swapping yarns. Since I need to spend one more night in Foggia, they advise me of the earliest train time, and thanking everyone I go to settle down in the tiny railway station. I have hardly dozed off, when two more family members arrive with meat, wine and fruit.

Everything is fresh and local. Having eaten some, I pack the rest neatly. Then they call again. The train is not due for an hour, would I like to have coffee with them? The family home is warmly welcoming, a simple set of rooms with several shrines and many family pictures. They take me round the corner to the tiny local chapel (usually locked). Delighted to meet a priest and pilgrim, they cannot do enough for me. When I try to find out about the area of 'Daunia', they give me a learned book which explains the complicated history of the area. To my delight, they dedicate it to me, all signing it. I have been entertained by angels.

Tuesday 19th August I get the earliest train back from Foggia and I'm on the road by 6.15 a.m. Having thought I would be walking on the flat, I find the road is straight enough but steep, and I'm impatient to get through to ancient Herdoniae. In this heat, that's a mistake, so I slow myself down by giving myself a task: to find out why almost everywhere round about is named Masseria followed by a nickname, Masseria La Quercia, Masseria San Marco, and each name seems to cover a large area.

In Castellucio dei Scauri there's a man in the cafe who knows. This was the way the whole plain of Puglia (the heel) and ancient Lucania (the instep) of Italy were divided between rich land owners, and to a large extent the system holds today. I'm trying to keep my mind active with little puzzles. and if the addled mind needs puzzles, the tired legs need motivation such as: "I think I can see a motorway maybe a mile away crossing the S.90. I'll rest under the shade of its concrete columns". Then the quessing-game. "Have I done one mile yet"? And the roadsigns will prove me right or wrong.

184

Then the road cuts across a railway line and I know I'm not far from Ordona. In this heat, 16 miles a day is my limit. Entering Ordona (a version of Herdoniae) I would sell my soul to the first inhabitant who would offer me an ice-cold drink. Providence intervenes. The people in the local food store apologise because their fridge has broken down. Never mind; water is water even if lukewarm, and they charge me twenty centesimi for a large bottle and I remain the undisputed owner of my soul.

No sense dragging myself round ruins, I'll visit Herdoniae tomorrow.

Wednesday 20th August. They told me in the village of Ordona that Herdoniae is on private property, but they spoke kindly of the landowner. This is the site of a 3000 year old settlement. What is visible is Roman and Byzantine.

Once I'm off the road and down the farm track a lady comes out to meet me, a Belgian who came here twenty years ago; she called in the professionals and a great dig began. She is delighted if visitors are interested in the outer wall, the small amphitheatre, the large forum.

Originally, she tells me, there was a local tribe, the Daunians. These were, of course, colonised by the Romans (who wasn't?) and Herdoniae became a Roman Municipium. She gives me a leaflet and encouragement to walk wherever I will. And I do, knowing that certainly Trajan walked on these stones. It is recorded that he personally supervised the planning of this new road, and this is a cross-roads and a key point in his scheme.

Perhaps I am being over-romantic, but since there is no-one to hurry me, I sit there for a long time taking it all in, and peopling the place with fleeing Daunians, marauding Romans, and his imperial self walking up and down, theodolite in hand.

Herdoniae has everything a ruined town could want, and I read its sorry tale of invasions and exile. They struggled on and as a Christian town it briefly flourished; it has a Byzantine basilica.

But finally, in the fifteenth century, the whole population met (eighty-three families they say), and decided to carry away all that was portable and found Ordona, a mile away which survives to this day, though it does not prosper

Back to my journey. It is a pilgrim route only in so far as pilgrims were glad to use this stretch, and Greeks or Lombards would protect them.

Along the road a hamlet, clean and modern, offers me provisions, and impulsively I buy a bottle of local wine to celebrate. We are now near the sea, though not near any port. For that, like the pilgrims, I shall have to turn south.

I mention hotels when they add something to my journey and so the Herdoniae at Passo d'Orta must be praised for its welcome, and one night's excellent cooking. It lies on its own in the flat lands, offering a surprising degree of comfort.

Here while sipping a glass of red or two, I read the local paper, where the great scandal is that the Mayor of San Giovanni Rotondo is being questioned about a huge grant given to improve the hotels in that place of pilgrimage.

Since San Giovanni has more hotels than Rimini, the sums are not small, and followers of Padre Pio will want to know that everything is as it should be.

Thursday 21ˢᵗ August. Today I wish to arrive at Ceringola which is only a name to me. Well, this is not difficult, a ten-mile walk, along a straight road. Very few cars pass me on the road, and as I climb up to the town. I cannot see a soul anywhere. It is eerie. I stand, mid-afternoon in a square beside a Roman milestone which is overshadowed by a huge municipal dustbin.

The digital sign outside a pharmacy (closed) gives, in sequence, time, date and temperature: (40° Celsius). The moving red digits are the only signs of life. But no. I can see a man in a bar, slowly wiping the marble counter. Is he the last survivor? I push open the door ready to greet him as my very own Man Thursday.

He does not even look up but continues wiping. "Buon Giorno," I say. Nothing. "Fa Caldo." Nothing.

"All right", I think. "I need you less than you need me"

I pivot on my left heel, crash the glass door and stand in the blazing square once more. The digital sign reads 41°.

I won't even look for a hotel in this tombstone of a town. (In fact, I can see one, covered in scaffolding.) Right! Back the way I came, to Passo d'Orta. I know where they'll make me welcome.

Only a mile into my angry retreat a local bus passes me, stops ahead, waits for me and offers me a lift, no question of a ticket. I've decided that today nothing is real. Best go along with it and accept this very Christian kindness.

Friday 22nd August. An early bus from opposite the hotel gets me back to Ceringola and the milestone. Now, as if by magic, the town has woken up. The chemist is affable and his sign says only 30°. Looking at my right eye for me he says that it is badly infected by the bite, and gives me an ointment with the encouraging prophecy that my left will soon be as bad, and that the damage is permanent.

I go quickly into the main square, whilst I still have eyes to see, and I find what I think is a prehistoric cemetery, huge clay pots sunk into the ground with square kerbs to protect them. So I sit down on a stone seat beside two old men with their black caps and walking sticks. "No, it's a granary", they say, and I go with them, and find that each family had its own storage jar. Ceringola is named after Ceres the goddess of grain and the harvest and it is still an important agricultural centre.

Canosa is my goal, a bit more than ten miles away. I've been there only once before, too briefly. It is visible from a long way off, crowning the hill. Between us lies the Ofanto River; once I get near I'll leave the modern road and cross by the Ponte Romano as they used to. If you want to preserve a historic site without making it into Disneyland, do as they've done here.

A narrow path crosses scrubland to the bridge which is restored and burnished, there's a mini park, a picnic area, tombstones and a Roman gate. Not many towns have as good an approach, though you have to leave the main road to find it.

The last mile is less attractive. Most suburbs are disappointing.

Saturday 23rd August. For two days I stay right opposite the cathedral at the Bohemund Hotel. I must ask to concelebrate in the eleventh-century church on Sunday, but I've promised myself first to visit the tomb of Bohemund. He was the elder son of Robert Guiscard who was the sixth son of Tancred de Hauteville. The Norman, knowing his property in France was not enough to be divided between twelve sons, told them to be off and make their own fortunes. What followed was the Norman Conquest not only of England but also of much of central Europe. Nothing was ever the same again. Bohemund played only a minor part. His mother Alberada was divorced for political reasons, though Robert did tell her that he still loved her. If you seek her tomb in secluded Venosa, not too far from here on the slopes of Monte Vulture, you will find it amongst the double ruins of a Norman and a Gothic church, one never quite demolished, the other incomplete. She insisted that they inscribe the words "Si genitum quaeres hunc Canusium habet" (If you seek my son, Canusium holds his corpse). I do seek her son, and will find him here in Canosa. It is a sad tale. He was brave and impetuous, but nearly always came off second best. As I approach the cathedral, I can see scaffolding down one side and so I am quite prepared for the notice barring entry to the public, which means I'll have to be patient, bide my time, look diffident but interested, and leave the rest to the kindness of the men working on site. Take it as done.

I had forgotten how sober are the bronze doors and (for now I am touching them) that they are not bronze but wooden, with bronze plates fixed to them. There are garlands and panelled scenes with the etched outlines of leading crusaders chatting amiably now and shaking hands, but 900 years ago they schemed every kind of treachery against each other. The workers signal that they are going to take a lunch break outside, and I stay on in the mausoleum alone with Bohemund. The square cell is now bare of furniture, but there is a bordered slab of stone set into the floor with BOAMUNDUS carved atop. Alone? No, because beside me on an upturned marble fragment sits that gentlest of travellers, Edward Hutton. About time that our paths crossed. He was last here ninety years ago, and I close my eyes and listen as he gives life to this unique building, this curiously oriental mausoleum. He tells me also that in the carve-up after the death of Robert Guiscard, Bohemund had to be content with the Terra di Otranto. By way of compensation he threw himself into the First Crusade, attacking Muslims and Greek Christians with equal relish, was himself twice prisoner of war, returned to Apulia to raise yet another army, caught fever and died. This is his memorial, a vast rectangular room surmounted by a pyramid which is set on an octagonal drum supporting a slender cupola. All in white marble and closed by those gates in Byzantine style.

I am grateful to share the moment with Hutton, himself so appreciative of the wisdom of the people who handed on local lore in the days when they still had the capacity to understand and transmit myth. One hundred years ago, Hutton made use of trains and trams, but also travelled fearlessly through bandit country. He had not the connections of an H. V. Morton but he wore his learning lightly and recorded what he heard in simple conversational style. I could listen to him for ever but the workers return. I give them thanks, and with a nod they let us into the south aisle of the cathedral. In the nave, we look up at both pulpits, knowing that all the area around would be open space for people to gather round to hear the Gospel or look up and listen to the preacher. The older pulpit is of marble. "By order of my Lord Suitbert the venerable priest"

We read: "Ego Acceptus Peccator Archidiaconus feci opus" (I Acceptus, the archdeacon, a sinner, did this work). Where have I seen that signature before, of the humble man who also did a great work? My companion Hutton mentions that he has just come from Monte Sant'Angelo, where likewise a proud eagle stands with claws resting on a human head, and a grinning feline face tops the spine of a marble missal-lectern. We then stand in awe of the ciborium over the altar, its four marble columns topped by a two-storied frieze of mini-columns. "Tomorrow", says the great traveller, "sit as near as you may to the bishop's throne". And he leaves me. A priest comes out of one of the confessionals, and I introduce myself. He cordially invites me to celebrate on Sunday.

Sunday 24th August That throne. It is supported by heavily tatooed twin elephants. There is nothing New Testament about elephants or eagles. The Hebrews, it is true, borrowed the eagle from the Babylonians for dramatic purposes. Since then militaristic nations have always loved them. The elephants are there for solidity and authority. This is a bishop's teaching chair. I listen to the preacher explaining the Gospel of the day. "Peter said, 'Lord to whom should we go if we left you?'" I sense a continuity of teaching here in this remote, forgotten, once-proud little town.

Monday 25th August My plan is to make eastwards for Andria and turn south as soon as I find the Appia Trajana. "Watch out for the Agricultural College", they say. "You can't miss it" As it happens it is the only group of buildings of any size on this route, so I turn right, because I know a Roman road when I see it, even when it is covered with tarmac. I say in Latin to a man who is just about to climb back onto his tractor, "Nonne haec via Appia Trajana est?" (Isn't this Trajan's Appian Way?) just as anyone in the ninth century from the foundation of Rome, when the road was built, might have done, and he confirms that it is, and he drives off down the road which the enlightened emperor built for him and for me. On either side of the road lie olive groves. It was not always so; this area once supplied grain for export. But now it boasts of the best olive oil in Italy (as do Tuscany and Sicily). Beneath the branches of the olive trees large nets are spread to catch the fruit as it falls. They'll have to wait a while, the olives are not mature yet.

My day's walk ends early at the crossroads. As I place five stones under the signpost I recall the words of the psalmist, "They have pierced my hands and feet, they have numbered all my bones".

Signposted to the right is the Castel del Monte which the Emperor Frederick, "Stupor Mundi" (Marvel of the world) built as a hunting lodge and which is an exercise in geometry mixed with the occult. Down the road I look and from past visits I remember its symmetry and its cosmic loneliness. Frederick spent very little time there, though his grandsons lingered longer. They were imprisoned by Charles of Anjou from their childhood onwards for thirty years in one of its eight towers, from which they looked out and saw this great road and all the coastline from the Gargano down to Brindisi. Much good the view did them.

I turn left to find a bed for the night in Andria. It is just three miles away, and I have not even decided whether to seek a lift, when a car draws up. This morning the driver offered me a lift just outside Canosa, but I explained then that I was walking. Now I am able to accept. He tells me there are two hotels in Andria, and puts me down near the *Dei Pini*. No trouble, they even have a proper bathroom at the end of the corridor.

Thursday 28th August. This morning I walk towards the crossroads. After two miles, a couple lean out of their car window and ask if this is the road for the Castel del Monte. "Go straight for about twenty kilometers", I say, "but first drop me at the *Appia*" and I am back on the old route. I love the views on either side. A flock of goat-like sheep, keeping close together wander into sight and seek the shade of an olive-grove. They are followed down by a shepherd who would not be out of place in one of those seventeenth-century nostalgic paintings by Claude Lorrain.

The *Appia* is not the only road going along the shore, and with the aid of notes I made earlier I think I can see the old drovers' road running slightly seaward, a hundred metres wide. Along this, oxen were driven back and forth seasonally between the Abruzzi and Apulia. But my road leads me to Corato, with its streets like a shady maze, to find at its heart the church of San Vito. Its original title was 'extra moenia' (outside the walls), but the city grew and engulfed it. The Knights of Malta owned the property and as I'm a pilgrim they owe me the coolness and shade given by its dome against the late morning sun.

I have no real desire to get back to the open road, but I wish to be early in Ruvo. I have no hotel booked but along the road I have seen plenty of adverts for the Talos, and signs lead me to it through the town. But I am deceived and annoyed to find that the Talos is shuttered, and is either being restored or demolished. Talos was a Greek hero, who by all accounts was given a rough time by the gods. Now I will have to telephone back and ask them to give me another night at the *Dei Pini* in Andria. Meanwhile, my reason for stopping here, the beautiful Cathedral of Ruvo, is a pilgrim's treat, and as I sit patiently outside waiting for the door to be opened, a little group arrives, a bride, a groom, a photographer and a couple of friends. I'm sure the wedding is neither here nor today, but the church front will make a nice backdrop for the photos, especially if you like griffins scowling over your shoulders and carved stone heads gurning and grinning in the background. We are on a minor loop of the railway which means I can get back to Andria by train. Out of the window I can see across the fields a monument marking where the Disfida di Barletta (Challenge of Barletta) took place in 1503. This tournament involved Spanish, French and Italian knights. There was more than one skirmish. At one point, the Spaniards fought the French, but for the showdown it was thirteen Italians against thirteen French. The Italians went first to Mass and then solemnly processed across the plain to a field half-way to Corato where, following every courtly custom, the ritual bloodbath took place. To this day, the Italians claim victory (and celebrate it as a tourist attraction), and the French admit that at the first shock seven of their knights were overthrown. However, they claim that the rest fought so bravely that the judges of the three nations declared a drawn battle. So, that's alright then. Comforted, I step down from the train at Andria, walk the short distance along the main street, and repair to my simple room and palliasse.

Friday 29ᵗʰ August. I go to pick up the five stones which I left last night to mark this stage. They have become reminders of the five wounds of Christ, in his hands and feet and side. In the accounts of the Passion, however, only the wound in Christ's side is mentioned. Though the psalm quoted does (in some translations) include the words "They have pierced my hands and my feet". And later Jesus did ask doubting Thomas to put his finger in the hole made by the nails. We do not know which variation of the gruesome Roman torture our Saviour endured. When did the devotion to the five wounds begin? It certainly appealed to the late medieval desire to share in the bloody suffering of Christ, but there was no crucifixion scene in fresco or in carving until the fifth century, no blood flowing until the twelfth century. St Francis of Assisi taught people to sense the sorrows as well as the joys of Christ. The 'Devotio Moderna' continued the process in the late fifteenth century. The Protestant Reformation was much more austere, but the Counter-Reformation boosted a tendency to wallow in the macabre, none of which is present in the sober Gospel narrative.

Today, once more, I stand on the steps of the church, and I decide not even to think of the heat, so early in the morning. Horace was disappointed with "Rubi" for his own reasons. (He was tired, and it was raining.) I love the monsters of the façade (they support columns) and the rose-window, set atop two arched windows. The church is neither large nor famous, but there is a sense of grandeur which must have made the pilgrims who took this slightly inland route want to stop and pray for a while. As I do. We are 900 ft.

above sea level, and this string of towns set back ten miles from the sea and the great ports is the line taken by those who sought Bari or Brindisi rather than the smaller more northerly ports.

Beyond Ruvo is Terlizzi. These have always been quite important little towns. 100 years ago, they had between twenty and thirty thousand inhabitants each, and with tourism they are doing well enough now.

You have to pick your way through the streets, which follow the contours of the hills they stand on. Here I don't even mind that the church is closed, the side porch accepts me. I am marking off the distance to Bitonto, 10 miles, and another 12 miles to Bari.

Once I'm back on the road, the traffic is just too much. This is one of the main cross-country roads to Bari. I resent the relentless stream of cars, and I keep well to the broad hard-shoulder beyond the white line. Here (and it has happened before) a couple of mindless idiots lean out and scream abuse at me, and no doubt they think they are the world's most subtle comedians. May they burst a tyre and land upside down in a ditch.

A sign for North Bitonto. Not far to go, and near the city centre is a plain and very ordinary hotel. They willingly offer me a bed for tonight. Expansion has not ruined this old city, the old centre is alive, and has not lost its character. Churches stand wall to wall with the houses of ordinary people. Washing hangs on lines. People chat in the streets and squares. I won't explore today. Instead I sit outside the Purgatorio, one of those churches which came late, after most of the pilgrims had already passed through. They exaggerated the elements of ghoulishness (skulls, demons, for example) which had begun to appear in the twelfth century. Purgatory, punishment and damnation. On its steps I read my evening prayer, "A terrore nocturno libera nos domine" (from the terrors of the night, free us O Lord). But high over the church door is something of ill omen; an Annuntiation with Gabriel coming in from the right. This is simply against all the rules of art and drama, pagan and Christian. Good news comes from the left. True the Della Robbia's went against this, possibly because their terracotta representations of the annunciation are reverse images of the original sketches.

Sunday 31ˢᵗ August. At my hotel in Bitonto, I sit down to breakfast: Cappucino with chocolate and a dry croissant. At my polite request the foaming cup it is replaced by a double espresso, and I am given some jam to soften the croissant.

First, a refreshing walk in the old town of Bitonto, whose churches would be famous were the town not off the beaten track. The cathedral with arcaded flank opens onto the market place. On the lintel of the main door are carved scenes from Matthew and Luke: the Annunciation, the Visitation, the Adoration of the Magi and the Presentation in the Temple. These were carved long before the rosary became popular. Above, in a lunette, is the Harrowing of Hell, where Christ, after his Resurrection, is shown, calling the great Old Testament figures to come up into Paradise; this is popular theology, a vivid dramatic expansion of a couple of lines in the New Testament.

Locals will have felt at home with the Annuntiation, and the Visitation; pilgrims will have waved to the intrepid Magi as they entered, and all of them will have been awed by the scene in the lunette, where Christ descends into hell to bring the ancient prophets to salvation. These local churches are alive with popular faith. Inside, the church has been saved from the worst excesses of the Baroque, and though it lacks the popular homely frescoes of Gospel stories or the Apocrypha, many capitals and sculpted supports remain. They are fresh, they are delicate. They are Arab-norman. So I sit beneath the pulpit to read my morning prayer, and I'm eager to make for Bari. I find that I'm walking urgently, faster than I need to. I'm in sight of my goal, the great port which has been my aim all these months. But I find nothing attractive about the horrible industrial wasteland, sprawling suburbs and looping roads on concrete stilts. I have to hope that under all this tarmac and concrete lies the hidden thread of the road once walked by pilgrims.

It is a commonplace that modern Bari is a disappointment with its straight but soulless streets, and that ancient Bari is a hell-hole steeped in crime. And yet I'm drawn to it again, for perhaps the tenth time in thirty-five years of travelling in Italy. First, I skirt the wall acknowledging the friendly warning of a stall-holder near the gate. 'Attento ai ladri!' 'Watch out for thieves!'

I do not enter immediately, but go to the shore. And here I am, and there is the Adriatic. To my right is the old port, and at least two shipping companies are ready to offer me safe and immediate passage to Greece. I am luckier than many pilgrims. For whole generations, Bari itself was closed to pilgrims, or the seas were not safe for travellers. Some pilgrims consoled themselves with visits to the substitute shrines here or in neighbouring towns, others set out north or south to find transport. But I breathe in the salted air, and tell myself. "It's true, I'm here, I've made it on foot". I take off my back-pack and pull my sweatshirt over my head, not in the manner of the triumphant footballer off whom the ball has bounced into the net, but because I wish to put on a clean shirt in order to greet St. Nicholas and thank him and all my fellow travellers for my safe arrival.

I can see his church through a gate and up a narrow street and I go into his square, sit on the steps of his shrine and look across at his statue. Children are playing, and out of the side streets people are slowly appearing and approaching the church for Sunday Mass. San Nicóla, San Nicolá, San Nicolo: on my journey I've heard all those forms of his name and each is right (or wrong) according to local tradition. Of the man himself, almost nothing is known. He was Bishop of Myra in Asia Minor in the fourth century. He prevented the death of three innocent men by bravely confronting a corrupt Roman Governor. He was probably imprisoned and perhaps martyred by the Emperor Diocletian. There you have it. Of the many legends surrounding him, Jacopo della Voragine (as always) has the best: that Nicholas was a rich man, and when his parents died, he wished to distribute his riches, but to God's glory, not his own. So when he found that a poor neighbour had three maiden daughters but no money, and that they were in danger of being forced into prostitution in order to obtain their dowries, then Nicholas secretly by night threw gold wrapped in a cloth into the house and in the morning the man rendered to God great thanksgiving and married his oldest daughter. After a while the servant of God once more threw in more gold, and the neighbour thanked God and the second was married but the neighbour decided to keep wakeful watch to know who had aided him and on the third occasion he caught sight of Nicholas who fled, but the neighbour caught up and knelt to him and would have kissed his feet; the holy man would not let him and bade him keep silent as long as he lived.

Sadly, the legend of St. Nicholas, with its message of selfless giving has been turned on its head, and the whole of society, Church and State now combines to promote selfishness and naked personal greed. In some places it is true St. Nicholas the bishop appears on December 6th with very simple gifts for children. But already his feast has been trampled into the ground by a fat drunkard in a red dressing-gown stampeding towards Christmas to destroy that feast too. Thus our children are encouraged to hold their own parents to ransom once a year, in the name of Christ.

Across the square I apologise to the saint, and as I begin rather stiffly to stand up to go in to Mass, I steady myself. I put my hand down and find it is resting on three coins which someone has let fall upon the church steps. "Grazie, San Nicola".

And so I take part in the Sunday Mass as one of the simple faithful. I want nothing more. But now I am distracted. Why go on pilgrimage at all? Pilgrims went on long journeys, by difficult and dangerous roads to pray at shrines to ask for special graces and to seek pardon for their sins. Some of these elements remain today, but the notion of pilgrimage has to contend with the blandishments of the tourist trade, the availability of cheap and fast travel and every other distraction. Somehow it survives. This

Mass is a pilgrim's thanksgiving. I remember that, whereas I had both travel and medical insurance, medieval pilgrims tended to rely on pilgrim saints, Christopher, Nicholas and others to get them there and back.

As Mass ends, I can see a group of people arriving and going down to the crypt. I shan't be alone in honouring St. Nicholas. Here, in most unlikely fashion, the theft of the bones of an eastern saint has united Greeks and Latins. St Nicolas seems to have the miraculous power of overcoming centuries-long and seemingly intractable differences.

Now that I've walked to Bari, I must surely go on to Santa Maria di Leuca, the furthest point on the peninsula. It isn't the most southerly point (look at the map. Italy leans to the left).

Tuesday 2nd September I take a last look at the old city which Horace dismissed as a fishing town. Wandering in the early morning through the narrow deserted streets of the old town, for once I can see not a single seller of contraband cigarettes (are there any legal cigarettes in Italy ?). Nor does anyone offer me drugs. I can see no-one whom I should avoid as a pick-pocket. A priest friend told me of his own experience, when his bag was stolen here. "Signore, i miei occhiali! Non che nient'altro di valore" (Sir, there's nothing of value there, but my spectacles)", he cried. Round the next corner his spectacles were left safely for him by a thief who had a heart, and would not leave an old man sightless. (Or was flattered to be called "Sir".) I sit once more in the Portico degli Pellegrini (the pilgrims' porch), and think of others who made the journey thus far towards Jerusalem, or who were on their way back from the Holy Land. Those who had made the perilous journey by sea had particular reason to be grateful to St. Nicholas. He was better than any insurance policy which merely recoups your losses (if you are lucky) whereas Nicholas brought you safely to port. It's a short step to the sea and to the *lungomare Augusto* (the seafront, named after the Emperor; they are well connected here). There is a pleasant walk alongside the city wall, which is fronted by grass and shrubs and faces the sea. The pier and fortress of St. Antony are dedicated not to the wonderworker of Lisbon and Padua, but to a saint who was popular 800 years before him, Antony Abbot and Hermit, Antony the Great. He inherited riches but gave everything away and went into the desert. He ate only once in two days, and his diet was bread, salt and water; he slept on bare rock, and endured temptations of the flesh. For years he lived alone, wrestling with devils, but his fame grew and he was persuaded to act as confessor to many, and as father to a community of cave-dwelling monks. During the persecution of Maximinian, he travelled to Alexandria, hoping (in vain) for martyrdom, but he counselled and emboldened those who were about to die. There are parallels with Padre Pio. His statue is always accompanied by a pig, though he himself never kept one, and he keeps a bell around his neck to ward off devils.

I find all this in a leaflet provided by the local church, as I sit on the sea-wall, looking out east, whence came the cult of so many early saints. The old port is so small. How did it cope with all the traffic of the great days of Bari during the crusades? The Mola di Bari is about fifteen miles away, so I shall have to walk slowly if I am to fill the day. The place-names are, San Giorgio, and Torre a Mare, The scenery is less than dramatic. Looking inland across the road and the railway-line which run side by side along the shore, I can see signs that the land is prosperous enough, and after a while, looking back I can see the headland and outline of Bari, and understand why it was so important with its wall and church towers and harbour. Every headland along this shore, right down to the last century was a godsend to sailors. Ahead of me is Torre a Mare, once a protecting fort, and I know I'm half way to Mola di Bari. Once this hamlet was a fishing port, and the nearest thing Bari has to a seaside resort. Mola, they tell me is of Greek origin. Here, once more the Emperor Trajan is honoured. The official entrance to the old city centre is through an arch named after him. It merges with nearby houses and is supported by columns made of Roman milestones. It is a monument to the importance of the road.

I'll make straight for the church of St. Nicholas, which was rebuilt by Dalmatian refugees in the sixteenth century. Along its flank is a beautiful porch, with caryatids supporting columns in the best of styles. There is enough left of the Romanesque church to remind me that this is not a brash newcomer. Here one beautiful thing grows from another. Whilst I'm sitting quietly the parish priest (may he be ranked amongst those who welcome pilgrims) comes over to me, thinking at first that I am a Franciscan who is due to arrive today. We exchange courtesies, which by stages turn into a conversation. When he hears of my journey he takes delight in answering my every question.

He shows me the carved font and the Holy Water stoop, and on the walls the story of Dalmatian Korkula and its sufferings. The two coastlines are so near that Italy was often the refuge of Balkan peoples fleeing the Turks.

This kindly priest, hearing of my interest in pilgrim saints, takes me out down the main street to an antique shop, where the owner, a sculptress is engaged upon restoring the local statue of St. Roch. The saint was with me on the day I made my lonely and tentative start at S. Rémy near the border, but what is he doing down here? He is being fitted for a dinky pair of silver booties, recycled from *ex votos*, that's what he is doing. We leave the shop together and continue our discussion over coffee and croissants. Knowing I intend to go to the furthest point of the peninsula the priest gives me the name of a Canon of the Cathedral of Otranto, who is an authority on its mosaics.

That's true hospitality, to send the traveller on with an introduction to others further down the road.

This is the sort of road on which you can't get lost, what with the sea being on your left, and the railway on your right. Every headland is occupied by a church and a fortress. Polignano a Mare is brilliantly simple, the town seems to grow directly out of the rocky headland. There is no knowing where the rock ends and the dwellings begin.

Monopoli which means "unique city" (remember, we're in Greece now), was refounded to take refugees from expiring Egnatia just down the coast. Egnatia dates from the Bronze age.

Monopoli suffered badly from Pirates, as also from Spaniards and Venetians. I can begin to see a pattern here. There must surely have been a route down the Adriatic from Venice, partly perhaps by land (some maps mark a *Via Francigena* just south of Venice) but most certainly by sea, for Venice at one time dominated the whole of the Adriatic. At certain times this route will have been much safer than the route down the western side of the Appenines which I have taken.

Monopoli today has no great pretensions, but its cathedral has a Byzantine picture of which they are proud. A woman at prayer tells me the story of the Madonna della Madia, which they say, floated ashore on a raft of thirty great beams, just at the time when they were transforming the cathedral from Romanesque to Baroque, the beams being just what was needed for the new roof. This is Mary Who Shows The Way. I'm not too proud to thank her for keeping me on track. There is another church, St. Mary of the Amalfitans. The warlike maritime Republic near Naples built its own church here. Each power-group wished to make a statement: "We're here, don't mess with us".

For this last short stretch, I shall keep to the *Appia*, but in addition I shall make short excursions inland to the towns set back from the coast, which were always part of the system. Give or take a tract or two, you can walk 360 miles from Rome to Brindisi, all on one named road, and think of all those who for various reasons used it, praised it or cursed it, but of necessity followed it. Here, starting the day in Monopoli, I ask to go into the sacristy, where in contrast to the heavy Baroque of the main church, they keep some bones of the old church, which died when they constructed the Baroque cathedral.

There are carved figures on a door-surround. Some may dare to call them primitive. Christ on the cross, carved as a child might carve him without knowledge of anatomy, but with a deep understanding of grace, and an instinct for telling a story with the minimum of detail. His right arm stretching down, falls into the arms of his Mother, his left, still nailed to the cross links us all to his saving act. The story moves from panel to panel and characters change places as they take on different roles. Devils and angels are spectators to the Gospel scenes and pious imagination takes us down with Christ to harrow hell and to bring back the good.

The port is still part of the town, and after all these centuries the castle still broods over it. Southwards along the coast, the shortest of stages, is the fortified Abbey of St. Stephen, about 900 years old, founded by the Benedictines, and later handed over to the Cistercians. At the heart of it is a Roman Tower which once defended the approach to Egnatia, which is one of the places I've had on my "must see" list for forty-five years.

Not far south I can see the carefully preserved site of San Stefano. To such a place even the Romans were newcomers. It was a border town between the Peuceti and the Messapi tribes, mere names now. But Egnatia is known to all as the town which Horace visited on the very last stage of his journey to Brundisium. In prehistory the land we now call Apulia was by no means remote. It was at the heart of the busy commercial and cultural life of the Mediterranean. Egnatia was known to Horace as Gnatia, and he passed through it on the very street I'm walking now, and as he approached the temple he made a merry quip to Maecenas about the incense which here was supposed to combust spontaneously on the sacred altar.

Pliny the Elder, in his *Natural Histories*, mentions a similar tale of wood catching fire by magic. Centuries later there were followers of another faith who, when the Spring Equinox arrived, rejoiced to see their priests emerge from a dark cavern bearing lights which had been kindled, they knew not how, and gave the cry "Alleluia". Horace is more sceptical than either Christian or Jew. "Let Abel the Jew believe it. Not I", he says. "Credat Judaeus Apella, non ego" Close as he was to Maecenas, chief financier and Ambassador Extraordinary to Augustus, perhaps even standing with him before this very temple, Horace laughs and says, "The gods are too busy to bother interfering in our daily lives".

Here is jovial yet erudite conversation, and at the moment I'm the only listener in this well-tended ruin of a little town on the Adriatic shore. There are other layers of interest, for Christians built a temple here, they who believe that God so cared that he sent his only Son to intervene, and the ruins of that later temple lie side by side with the other. And when the day of reckoning comes, will the followers of that later cult be welcomed into bliss, and the genial Horace be excluded? Not if there be any justice on such a day.

The main road, the one used by the friendly Horace, runs right through the centre of the town, and, having transport, they will have reached Brundisium in a day, but I shall take longer as I wish to go the whole way on foot.

I first take a rest upon the shore, and sit on the headland, looking with wonder at the rough-shaped limestone blocks which might have been colonised and ruined by tourists but have been spared because we, in a reversal of history, no longer think of Apulia as a crossroads.

If ever you are going for a long walk, then, as you cross the finishing-line, do not stop dead, but continue as long as the urge to keep walking remains. It is the body's way of winding down. And the mind's way too.

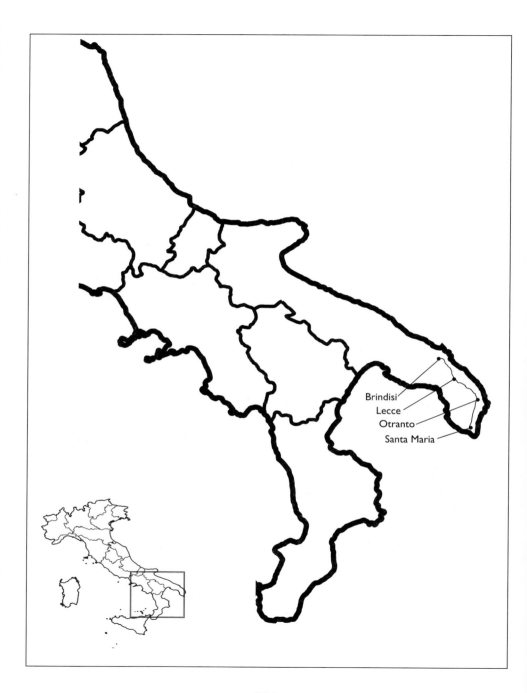

Brindisi
Lecce
Otranto
Santa Maria

Epilogue

So I decided to walk on to Saint Mary at the End of the World ('St. Mary of the White Cliffs' as the Greeks called it), and then to Otranto, because it was the end of the road for so many. Between Saturday 13th September and Saturday 27th I made the journey and explored the peninsula. On foot, because I felt there was no other way of continuing.

The Salento peninsula, stiletto heel of Italy, is like a great limestone pier jutting out into the heart of the Mediterranean. Long ago it was a lively centre of commerce between continents, so the pier has many mooring-points. For ships from Sicily it offered the double-safe harbour of Taranto. Further south the 'beautiful city' of Gallipoli smiled a welcome to all. From the Levant a permanent way was ploughed to and fro through the waters to Brindisi and Otranto, though the east coast also suffered horribly from piracy and pillage.

For Italians "Fare un Brindisi" is to drink to a toast, and I was in the mood to do so as I stood at the top of the steps between the two columns which mark the official end of the Via Appia, even if I was also sobered by the thought that the dying Virgil was carried up those same steps as he returned from a diplomatic mission in Greece. For a fortnight I walked down the centre of this lively pier, and listened and learned. Between Brindisi and Lecce I visited Squinzano and Trepuzzi and lingered because of the poetry of their names, which rivals that of Northumbrian villages such as Pity Me and Tow Law. I was walking alongside the magic railway which radiates from Lecce, that city being the pier's central attraction, a fairground of Baroque art. Lecce gives a new meaning to the word 'unique'. Approaching from the north, I felt I had to stop once more at the cemetery, as good a place as any to begin a visit to any Italian town or village. You meet the ancestors. In the midst of the graves the Norman convent has a cloister, and solid church structure which have not yet quite been devoured by the Baroque overlay of weird carvings which cover columns and walls in the way that mushrooms colonise a venerable oak.

Next I began to circle the city wall, but soon I could not resist the lure of the little church of the Rosary, and I went in. There are carvings which might more fittingly be found in the gardens of Tivoli. Statues which may be Christian in name but in shape and inspiration are totally pagan. Here in each church façade the sparrow has found a home and the pigeon a nest to place their young. Why do carvings overflow every ledge? Why are columns crowned with ruffs? Why are there ornate vases everywhere? I don't know, but it is value for money. Thank you, Lo Zingarello! (the little gypsy). And why is it, by the way, that all the churches here were creations of architects with operatic names, and most of them locals too?

The Duomo and the seminary are centred on a square which calls out for actors to people it. In recent times, the main square has had open heart surgery to reveal a Roman amphitheatre. The great emperors of the second century A.D. would have destined Lupiae to live for ever, but that was not its fate.

Goths, Greeks and Normans chased each other howling across the boards, as the great Saint Oronzo looked down on all this from the height of his column (stolen from Brindisi). I go down a prosperous street of shops to the shamelessly glorious Santa Croce. Riccardi began it, Zimbalo added three portals and then called in his nephew Zingarello. The square is too narrow, you cannot step back far enough to get a frontal view, so in effect you are sitting in the front row leaning back and looking up at the stage, where there is much going on, some of it related to Christianity.

For Leccese Baroque think Chocolate Fudge, and of someone who has taken great pains to decorate the cake. When Craufurd Tait Ramage arrived here in 1828, he had travelled on his own through the Campagna, Calabria and Puglia. Spain at the time dominated the Kingdom of the two Sicilies, and bandits terrorised these remote regions. With the proverbial umbrella and a stout heart this twenty-four-year-old Scottish Presbyterian went fearlessly everywhere "in search of ancient remains and modern superstitions". He found plenty of both, but of Lecce he said, "No ancient remains are visible, nor, indeed, is there anything to interest a stranger". Oh well, I don't blame the likeable man.

South of Lecce I saw a sign for Calimera. Imagine the joy of waking up each morning in a village called 'Good Morning'. As a second best I lingered there for a coffee, and asked the cafe owner if the place was still Greek. He took me over to the Pharmakon (Chemist's), and pointed out a notice written in Greek characters (I saw others later). A shop window had an advertisement for a Zenodocheion (a Youth Hostel, I understand from the description). 'Good day to you, little village. May you never change'.

At Maglie, the welcome was such that I ought to mention the Rhodia Hotel which is just the right distance for visiting both Santa Maria and Otranto. Here I saw a tomb inscribed "Mortem non mortuum devorat sepulchrum". It beats the rubbish they're starting to offer you on the internet as 'suitable for funerals'. The tomb marks an end, not of the corpse, but of death itself.

Here I made a choice, to go straight for the finishing post, at Santa Maria de Finibus Terrae (Saint Mary at the end of the world). After that Otranto would be the conclusion of my pilgrimage. The heat was such, and the villages so ordinary, that I have little memory of the journey, except for two encounters. First, I was stung in the throat by a bee at Scorrano, and thought it was best to get the sting out at all costs. When the bleeding didn't stop, I became concerned and went in to a herbalist who advised a cortisone injection. No thanks. I walked on, and also survived. In the last mile before the cape, on a completely deserted road, I realised I was being followed by a weirdo who overtook me and danced in front of me without benefit of trousers like a faun straight from the Etruscan scenes of D.H. Lawrence. I was preparing to climb over a stone wall and make for the nearest cottage when he finally got the message that I was not interested in anything he could offer me. Well every faun is entitled to his *après-midi*, I suppose.

Now I could see the Lighthouse, and the shrine of Santa Maria. In 1828 Tait Ramage arrived, of his visit he wrote:

> at the hour when Mass was to be performed. I was of course expected to attend. I told them I was an Englishman and that my principles did not admit of my joining in their form of worship. I could stop, however, till my muleteer performed his religious duties and would meanwhile descend to the shore to admire the works of the great God whom we both worshipped, though under different external forms. This pleased the old man [the priest] who could not but see that I had some tincture of religion and he said that he would pray that I might see the error of my ways, to which I replied that I had been taught in our own heretical country that the prayers of a righteous man availeth much.

I too arrived in time for Mass, and I went in. There was an African bishop presiding at the Mass and when devotions were completed I went with other pilgrims to greet him. It was the Archbishop of Masaka, so I told him I had seen photographs of a school and a hospital in his diocese which had been renovated by the efforts of the parishioners of Manor House, Hackney. He asked me to thank them. I never felt so Catholic as at that moment. Conversation had been in English, and an Australian pilgrim saw fit to compliment me on my command of the language. Santa Maria is not the furthest point on the peninsula. I went on one mile to Punto Ristola. Now I could look back and see the white cliffs. 'Leukos' in Greek means 'white', hence Santa Maria de Leuca. I could go no further. I took off my trainers and set them on a rock and photographed them, in order to send back an image to the dear old friend who had bought them for me.

I had reached yet another goal but overall, I suppose I was disappointed. This place was nothing like the end of the world. Then I thought of Land's End, in Cornwall, and of what they have done to it, and I knew I was better off here.

ÓTRANTO

From Maglie to Otranto is a very short walk and this was my third visit to this magical city which is the last word in Christian mythology. Unfortunately it is best known as the mispronounced title of a novel, *The Castle of Otránto*, by Horace Walpole. At first sight it is a walled city with a castle, set by the sea. It tries not to be overwhelmed by the cheap end of the Greek ferry trade.

Centuries ago its narrow stone-clad streets would delay any invader whilst the inhabitants tried to escape. Today there was no one about, except that the Byzantine church of St. Peter was open for prayer. Here I was happy to revere fragments of frescoes, very domestic, and to sit turn by turn in its round-apsed chapels. For just a few seconds I was in sole possession of a place which has hardly ever been safe from invaders. I was simply delaying the moment when I would visit the most mysterious Cathedral in the World. If you wish to take me up on that, visit it first. (Preferably after a 900 mile journey on foot.) Back at Mola di Bari, the parish priest had mentioned Don Grazio Gianfreda, who was for nearly fifty years parish priest of the cathedral at Otranto. He is the expert on the famous mosaic floor. I have a little booklet written by him.

First, I stood in the square and looked up critically at the plain façade the over-ornamental doorway and the delicate rose-window. Once inside I was no longer in charge, and I knelt on the carpet which had been rolled out to welcome me, as it has been for every pilgrim for 800 years, at least when it was not being trampled on by the horses of Muslim invaders, or obscured and damaged by the totally unnecessary wooden benches of latter-day Christians, who do not understand the purpose or function of a church. There are three mosaic carpets covering the nave and the two aisles, the work of the priest Pantaleone The story of salvation is told without false divisions of the sacred and the profane. Alexander the Great is proud to be in the company of Atlas. Rex Arturus (King Arthur) waves to Cain and Abel as he rides by. The pictures are in a naïve and lively style common in Puglia. The human forms are similar to the figures on the Bayeux tapestry of a century before, and I suppose there is a mixture of Byzantine and Norman in it. There is no attempt to be realistic, as the Renaissance had not yet been invented, nor are there any unnecessary divisions between earth and heaven, or pagan and Christian. There is a healthy preoccupation with the seasons, which have their star signs as markers.

There is the most charming little Noah's ark, and a Tower of Babel which could sue Leggo for breach of copyright. Have they dared to miss out Jonah? No, there he is right at the top of the apse being thrown out to the fishes, while the King of Niniveh is busy rending his garments as a timely sign of repentance. In one aisle is shown the close link between religion and the world of nature. Naively-drawn goats and lions mingle with harpies and dragons. The Mosaic of the Last Judgement delights in the horrors of Hell. Angels weigh up the souls of the dead. A bound captive stands before King Satan, and for our consolation, the soul of a good man who is saved stands, arms upraised, in the familiar pose of the Orante. It is possible that every figure in this marvellous floor has a cousin in Ravenna, Rome or Calabria. What is so thrilling it that they are all gathered here, not preserved but living. It was almost too much to cope with. I went over towards the sacristy where I could see and hear a group of clerics talking quite loudly. Politely, I hesitated before entering. Conversation was animated, and one robust silver-haired canon suddenly cried "Per Bacco!" to emphasise a point, exactly as a pagan priest might have done when this same spot was dedicated to the pagan gods. I heard the same expression thirty years ago from the lips of a cardinal when he and I were guests of Don Serena, a parish priest, and the wine of the Val D'Arda provided the spark.

A hesitant cough seemed in order. "Is it possible to salute Don Grazio?", I said. "Certainly, but certainly! He's near the skulls, preparing a marriage for that young couple". Don Grazio was in the doorway of the chapel of the martyrs, where the walls are lined with glass cases full of the skulls of the victims of a massacre in 1480 when the whole city was devastated by the Turks, in the time when violent wars crashed back and forth across these straights. Don Grazio was an old man, but immediately answered my tentative call by rushing across, vaulting a low bench on the way to clasp my hand. "You made it", he said, remembering that three weeks ago the parish priest of Mola di Bari had told him I might possibly come here.

Naturally I began to question him on the Mosaic. In no time he brought me into the sacristy, and from the bookstall gave me a large heavy book, his *magnum opus*, which summarises all the many books he had written on Otranto and its mosaic floor. He signed it there and then.

"Have you seen them?", he asked, looking across the basilica to the mosaics.

"I've just begun", I said.

"You'll never finish", he replied. " But do not forget the crypt."

I mentioned to this erudite man that during the last two weeks I had felt I was not walking towards a remote place or towards the end of the world. He put his hand on mine and looked into my eyes. "Otranto", he said, "was the Gibraltar of the Adriatic." Don Grazio, during his time as parish priest (since 1956) had been a second Pantaleone and overseen the rescue and restoration of this incomparable work of faith and by being there, day by day, had come to understand it better than anyone else in the world. Felix homo.

We parted, and I did as he had counselled me; I went down into the crypt, a little forest of re-used pagan columns, a cave, a womb. And there I fell asleep.

> A l'alta fantasia qui mancò possa;
> ma già volgeva il mio disio e 'l velle,
> sì come rota ch'igualmente è mossa,
> l'amor che move il sole e l'altre stelle.
> (Dante Paradiso. Canto XXXIII)

> At this point power failed high fantasy
> but, like a wheel in perfect balance turning,
> I felt my will and my desire impelled
> by the Love that moves the sun and other stars.